Getting It All Together

The Heritage of Thomas Merton

Getting It All Together

The Heritage of Thomas Merton

By

M. Basil Pennington, O.C.S.O.
Amiya Chakravarty
David Steindl-Rast, O.S.B.
Richard Anthony Cashen, C.P.
George Kilcourse

Edited By

Timothy Mulhearn

 Michael Glazier, Inc.

Wilmington, Delaware

First published in 1984 by Michael Glazier, Inc., 1723 Delaware Avenue, Wilmington, Delaware 19806 • ©1984 by Cistercian Abbey of Spencer, Inc. All rights reserved • Library of Congress Card Catalog Number: 83-82937 • International Standard Book Number: 0-89453-380-0 • Cover design by Gibby Perry • Typography by Robert Zerbe Graphics • Printed in the United States of America

CONTENTS

CONTRIBUTORS

RICHARD CASHEN, C.P., was ordained for the Passionist community in 1966. He received an M.A. in theology from Saint Michael's in Union City and an M.R.E. from Fordham University. In 1972-73 he studied at the Institute for Spirituality at the Gregorian University in Rome and earned a doctorate in theology, *summa cum laude*, with his dissertation, *The Concept of Solitude in the Thought of Thomas Merton*, which has since been published by Cistercian Publications. Fr. Cashen has taught at Assumption College and has been involved in formation work since 1968.

Poet, author and scholar, friend of Gandhi, Schweitzer and Merton, DR. AMIYA CHAKRAVARTY has contributed greatly to a mutual understanding of East and West. He received his M.A. in philosophy from Patna University in India, his doctorate from Oxford University in 1937, and was the first Asian to be elected senior research fellow at Oxford. Dr. Chakravarty has taught on many campuses in several countries; since 1967 he has been at the State University of New York's College of New Paltz, where he is now professor emeritus of philosophy. He has contributed to various Merton activities and was consulting editor for *The Asian Journal of Thomas Merton*.

GEORGE KILCOURSE is a priest of the Archdiocese of Louisville, Kentucky. He earned his Ph.D. from Fordham University and has written on the christological themes and the poetry of Thomas Merton. Fr. Kilcourse is asso-

ciate professor of theology at Bellarmine College in Louisville, and is also a consultant to the Archdiocesan Office
of Ecumenical Affairs.

M. BASIL PENNINGTON, O.C.S.O. is a Cistercian
(Trappist) monk of the Abbey of Our Lady of St. Joseph
in Spencer Massachusetts where he entered in 1951 after
graduating from Cathedral College, Brooklyn. After
ordination in 1956 he spent several years in Rome gaining
an S.T.L. *cum laude* from the Pontifical University of
St. Thomas Aquinas and a JCL *summa cum laude* from the
Gregorianum. He assisted at the Second Vatican Council
as a *peritus* and in the preparation of the New Code of
Canon Law. With Thomas Merton he started Cistercian
Publications in 1968 and founded the Institute of Cistercian
Studies at Western Michigan University in 1973. Father
became nationally known through his efforts to help the
American Church refind its contemplative dimension
through Centering Prayer. For four years he served as a
vocational father, lectured widely and published a book
on vocational discernment. Father has published over a
dozen books and some 300 articles. Currently he has been
writing and speaking more on peace and social justice.
He is preparing for publication a personal study of Thomas
Merton.

BROTHER DAVID STEINDL-RAST was born in
Vienna, where he studied art, anthropology and psychology.
He holds degrees from the Vienna Academy of the Fine
Arts and the Psychological Institute, and received his Ph.D.
in experimental psychology from the University of Vienna.
In 1953 he joined the newly-founded Benedictine monastery
of Mount Saviour in Elmira, New York, where he received
formal training in philosophy and theology. While still
a monk of Mount Saviour, Brother David has founded the
Benedictine Grange in West Redding, Connecticut. With
a deep concern for contemporary monastic spirituality
and for the contribution of Thomas Merton, Brother David
has lectured and written extensively. He is also co-founder
of the Center for Spiritual Studies, established by Bud-
dhists, Hindus, Jews and Christians.

EDITOR'S NOTE

"So I will disappear." Thomas Merton concluded his Bangkok talk—the final talk of his life—with this sentence. As he died only a few hours later, Merton's unintended "prophecy" was quickly fulfilled in one literal sense. When we consider what he left behind, however, we can only conclude that in a very real way Thomas Merton is still among us. What gives witness to this fact is the ever-increasing number of symposia, conferences, books and articles which use his life, writings and thought as prisms through which to view the world. The papers in the present volume are from a series of Merton Symposia conducted at the Seminary of the Immaculate Conception, Huntington, New York, during the years 1975-1978.

Clearly, no single work can present a reader with the entire heritage of Thomas Merton. This man, this monk-priest-author, left far too rich a corpus of written works to be so easily digested. In assembling the collection offered here there was never any consideration of putting forth a complete assessment of Merton; rather, the intention has been to share a limited number of thoughts and insights with an audience and readership seeking guidance in interpreting and understanding the world in which we live.

My personal favorite Merton book is *The Silent Life*, in which the author gave an insider's view of the monastic life. It was into this life of hidden prayer, work and study that Merton first "disappeared," becoming Fr. Louis, of the Trappist Abbey of Our Lady of Gethsemani. But that proved to be no more a disappearance than did his *transitus*, twenty-seven years later. From within the monastery there came forth a stream of writings which transcended national, cultural and religious boundaries and distinctions, and which has had a profound effect on the spiritual lives of an untold number of people.

I think Merton's posthumously published *Asian Journal* is a fitting last work, for in it can be found woven together various threads which appeared in other writings. The Catholic priest living the Rule of St. Benedict shares his faith with his brother- and sister-followers of that Rule; at the same time, the Trappist monk is able to share with Buddhist monks the common elements of their monastic lives. These twin aspects capture something which is of the essence of Merton's thought. Firmly rooted in the teachings and the traditions of the Catholic Church, he saw in all religious traditions the human longing and search for the transcedent.

That Thomas Merton was so firmly rooted in his faith provides another key to the heritage he left us. A person who is so well-anchored can appreciate tradition and yet look for new expressions of that tradition. Such a person can say, "Let us express our tradition in a contemporary idiom. We know the value of what we believe; let us ask new questions and shed new light on our every-growing tradition so that we may share it with others in a constantly evolving present." Intellectually Merton never stood still. Yet he was not just blown about by the ever-changing winds of transitory fads. He teaches us that a solid appreciation of the past is a requisite for understanding the present and for true growth in the future.

In order to grow in the spiritual life one must confront oneself in one's relationship with God. The monk, by his very life hidden with God in the monastery, is the public witness to this truism. It would lead to a very short-lived society were we all to embrace the monastic life, yet the many outside the monastery can learn much from the few within. The cloistered monk and nun give witness to the value of solitude. This solitude is not an aloneness in any negative sense. Rather, it is a unitive force because as discrete persons each of us develops a personal relationship with God. Being related to him, we are related through him to a wider society.

Those who grow in their spiritual lives are often given the grace of being able to communicate this to others. Merton had this gift of communication and was able to express himself and his ideas not only in his prose but also in his poetry. I must confess that I have to struggle to appreciate poetry. Yet to those whose intellects and imaginations are more finely tuned than my own, Thomas Merton's poetic expression has found wide appeal. A measure of his heritage is his ability to reach people in multiple ways.

Sociologists and others who measure and report contemporary social phenomena cite an increase in the felt importance of religion in the lives of Americans in the mid-1980s. When compared with popular feeling a decade prior, more people now believe that religion, rather than science, holds the ultimate answers to life. To this growing segment of the populace the heritage of Thomas Merton has a particular relevance.

As a monk, a priest and an author Merton did much to interpret values—monastic values and religious values (the two overlap, but are not synonymous)—to all who would read his works. However, those interpretations are only a part of his heritage, for they are the product of an individual situated within a particular context with its own frame of reference.

The other part of his heritage transcends that context. He teaches us to be traditionalists on the one hand, but on the other, to be open, to ask, to probe, to grow. It is in the spirit of wanting to share this multifaceted heritage of Thomas Merton, Fr. M. Louis, O.C.S.O., that the present volume is offered.

Timothy Mulhearn

INTRODUCTION

M. Basil Pennington, O.C.S.O.

In 1946, Thomas Merton (Father Louis, O.C.S.O.) translated an official report of the General Chapter of the Cistercians of the Strict Observance (Trappists) entitled: *The Spirit of Simplicity. Characteristic of the Cistercian Order.* He included a selection of texts from Saint Bernard and a commentary of his own. The true monk is a simple man. This was one characteristic that Merton himself evinced to a remarkable degree. The witnesses are many, even apart from the self-disclosure in his writings.

Frank Dell 'Isola, who has prepared the most complete bibliography of Merton's writings, says in describing his first meeting with Tom: "He quickly puts you at ease; there isn't anything pompous, artificial, or affectatious in his demeanor. He talks and smiles like a small boy, but there is fire and determination in his words and actions. Yet his simplicity is overwhelming."

I would say the same thing. There comes to my mind a wonderful picture I have of Tom. It was given to me by Gene Meatyard. Gene had just given Tom his first camera, and then snapped this candid shot. Tom is quite literally smiling from ear to ear, the pure glee of a child on Christmas morning.

There are two kinds of simplicity: a simplicity of fullness and a simplicity of lack. The latter is pitiful, whatever its cause; sadder when it is due to one's own failure to develop the rich potentialities of life. The former in its fullest is

God, who is absolute simplicity, all that is, in its perfection and utmost beauty. It is towards a simplicity of fullness that we all strive. The chapters in this volume share the witness and wisdom of Merton in regard to such an integration.

Looking from the outside, even to the end, Merton was indeed a paradox. Just a few days before his death, at a time when he was in search of the highest wisdom of the East and having one of his most profound experiences of integration at Polonnaruwa, he was still visiting bars and enjoying the luxury of five-star hotels in the midst of the abysmal poverty of the subcontinent. When I took a friend to dinner at the Galle Face Hotel in Colombo to see where Tom stayed these last days, my guest, a native, said the price of our dinner would keep his family for a month or buy him a fine custom-made suit. How did this monk, dedicated to being "poor with the poor Christ" and so socially conscious, put it all together? The reflections in this volume give us some elements of the answer, an answer affluent American Christians desperately need as they become more and more aware of the reality of their global citizenship and responsibility.

One of the authors here was with Merton just days before his death; another spent some very precious days with him on the eve of his flight to the East. It is fitting that the first chapter in this volume is by a man from the East. Merton disappeared into the East. His journey thence began intellectually and spiritually some years before his physical take-off from San Francisco. In this journey, Tom, who is the greatest spiritual writer we have known in this century, has gotten too far removed from many of us in the West. We need someone to bring him back to us. Amiya Chakravarty is a good man to do it. A son of India, he has lived long in the West. He knew Tom for many years and was with him on his eastward journey both intellectually and, in the last days, physically.

Brother David Steindl-Rast well takes up where Chakravarty leaves off, for he is a man of the West, though no western monk has so completely and effectively reached out to the East. During those October days at Redwoods, just before Merton flew East, David had an opportunity to gather up Tom's emerging thoughts on this integration. He later published them in his article "Reflection on Thomas Merton's Last Days in the West." They help him as he interprets for us some of the most significant passages of the *Asian Journal*.

Richard Cashen finally locates us solidly back to our familiar Western terrain with his careful analysis of some of Merton's earlier writing when, as Father Louis, he talks about the space of solitude that opened for him the way to integration. Under Merton's tutelage, Cashen learned that "true solitude sends us into the world with a new vision, new motivation, new dynamism, to be Christ's leaven in the world and to incarnate his love in our time, in our place."

Perhaps the starting point for us to discover the value and beauty of integration and our need for it has to be in the East. We in the West have gotten so locked into our heads, so trapped in our concepts and conceptual knowledge. However, Father George Kilcourse suggests that there is another route, one quite present in the West, and one that Merton employed: the way of poetic insight and experience.

Ultimately, though, there is only one complete and adequate expression of integration and that is a Person, the Second Person of the Blessed Trinity, the Incarnate God, Jesus Christ. This is the way Merton—with all his openness to the wisdom of other peoples, cultures and religions, and even to the secularist—ultimately saw it. Christ remained ever the focus of the integration about which he wrote and for which he strove, the integration which comes about in its fullness only through unity with God and all others: "Whatever I may have written, I think it can all be reduced in the end to this one root truth: that God calls human persons to union with Himself and with one another in Christ, in the Church which is His Mystical Body."

In 1973 I had the privilege of chairing an international Symposium at Oxford University. It was a meeting of the Christian East and West. In the course of the frank exchange, representatives of both traditions admitted to a current dearth of spiritual fathers and mothers. I asked one of the Orthodox bishops what they do in the face of this fact. Bishop Antonie replied that when one cannot find a spiritual father in the flesh he turns to the Fathers. They are indeed alive in the Lord. Through their writings we can sit at their feet and receive today the needed "word" of life. Merton lives. The men who have shared their thoughts and experience in this book know that, for they know him. May their sharing not only give us more insight into a central facet of Merton's heritage, but also invite us to sit at the feet of the greatest spiritual father of our century so that he can personally help us to get it all together.

We live in a time of maximum, unprecedented and imminent peril. At any moment our civilization could be wiped out. The course we are presently pursuing, which Merton foresaw only too well, can but lead to extinction. If the whole is not consumed in a holocaust, it will be wasted on a perilous pile of nuclear debris that will contaminate whatever else remains. We have to find security in another direction and soon. The shift begins, as Merton never tired of asserting, with personal conversion, from the fragmented and therefore very vulnerable and defensive self to the true self in God, in communion with all creation. Only when enough of us attain a degree of integration, by whatever path—in his last talk Merton did not rule out even Marxism as being at least initially a way—can our global community be integrated so that we can pursue together the well-being of the entire human family.

The spirituality to which Merton here invites us through these his friends and interpreters is a way of prayer that is beyond prayers and even exercises of prayer. It is a state of essential prayer—a prayer of being, a being in communion, a full expression of the Incarnation in us. There is much more to what Merton says and what these authors say under his inspiration than is perceived in a simple reading. It is only when we respond to this heritage and experience getting it together that we will know the full power and import of the ultimate teaching of this great spiritual master of the West. Fortunately Thomas Merton has left us a very abundant and real literary heritage through which he can now speak to us. From almost any starting point he can lead us step by step along the way he knows by experience, to the full simplicity of integration.

At Polonnaruwa, before the reclining Buddha, Father Louis attained a certain completeness, and yet at the bottom of the post card he sent me two days later from Singapore he wrote: ". . . magnificent so far & more to come." There is always more till we come to all the fullness of the simplicity of God, which is touched here only in moments of transcendent enlightenment, but is meant to be ours forever in Christ in the fullness of the Body in the Kingdom to come.

It is my hope that the publication of this volume will invite many to choose Father Louis as a spiritual father, and to pursue with him that task of getting it together, which will lead to the full simplicity of God, the source of the unity and fraternity of the human family.

1

TRUE RELIGION: EXPERIENCE AND RELATION

Amiya Chakravarty

We are all children of the same family. We belong to the one universe which is ours. The whole adventure of man on this planet is one single adventure of human life, of all that gives meaning and purpose. There are, however, differences which are real. This is the basic problem in spiritual culture, religion, and aesthetics: how to draw a line between divisions that are illegitimate and differences that are genuine; the problem of the individual and the all-embracing universal. They are not mutually exclusive. That which is unique is unique. Only through the individual uniqueness can we achieve the universal, but if we separate that which is unique from the universal, we fall into error. The universal is the whole divine plan; the meaning of life, tenderness, compassion, mercy, grace, beauty, and character—all these belong to the span of Truth.

There must be a fundamental meeting of civilizations and religions. This is taking place now a little more than before. In India the idea of wholeness of the universal being found in every individual part is illustrated in many ways.

There was a great sage in the Vedic period, one of the loftiest minds we have known in our spiritual literature. To him many disciples came to gain an understanding of the nature of reality. Once he was asked, "How can I see God?" He replied: "Bring me a bowl of water." The disciple did so. "Bring me some salt." Again the disciple obeyed. "Pour that salt into the water in the bowl. Where is it now? It is invisible, it is gone. Now, taste the water from this edge of the bowl. How does it taste?" "Salty." Taste it from the other side." "Salty." "So it is with the pervasive reality of the Divine. God is in the whole of the universe even as the salt is in the whole of the water."

We can discern the salt in the water; we can touch the Divine at any point of the universe. If we do not sense the handiwork of the Creator, if we do not feel it, we are separating the Creator from his creation. We have defiled and polluted and wronged the Divine gifts. But still his touch is on the fields and the sky, rich in color and beauty, and we are filled with wonder.

Once I asked my students, "Coming up the hill to the college, what did you see?" "Nothing special," they replied. "But didn't you see those dandelions? They are perfect—yellow, beautiful, every petal curled. It needed all the power of gravitation, of solar energy, of the chemical resources of the earth—you might say the whole anvil of creation—to create each dandelion. And you say you saw nothing!"

If we are so unobservant, so ungrateful, how can we feel the shock of the Divine? Only through specific circumstances? Of course we do that, too. We are alerted by a tremendous experience, a spiritual opening. But the Divine handiwork is there, in the green grass. All the time we are doing everything possible to destroy the innocent gifts of life, but we do not succeed. The grass grows green again, the sky blue. If our pollution, our sinfulness, disturbed the whole chain of the universe, that would indeed be tragic, but it doesn't.

The total harmony of existence is in every religion, unmistakably there. Someone who wanted to know the mystery of life asked: "Where is it?" A sage replied: "Do you see those acorns under that great oak tree?" "Yes, there are quite a few." "Bring me one of them." He did so. The sage continued: "Bring me a sharp knife. Cut off the first layer. What do you see?" "A green underneath." "Cut it again." The inquirer went on cutting. "Where is the oak tree?" asked the sage. The inquirer did not find it, but the oak tree was there in the acorn.

Hidden, the very meaning of existence, the wholeness, scattered in minute particles of Divine power, there is an infinitude. It is not a question of worshiping stock and stone, or saying that Shiva is sitting on a mountain in the Himalayas and we have just to bow our heads to a particular rock and God comes to us. That is not so. There is a meaning which is somehow transferred through human adoration to the power we have of giving shape to our visions. And this, of course, is not only Indian or Asian. One can see it in Michelangelo. Not satisfied with the block of marble that was given him, he went to the quarries and sought the particular stone that he needed. He already knew the kind of chisel he would use. When he got his stone he could turn it into a Pieta. What was the power that gave him the vision and the specific knowledge, control, and discipline?

Vision alone is not enough. We sometimes think that an actual vision will give us the needed power. None of the great epochal changes take place without persistence. Doctor Salk and his associates pursued the virus of polio for years and years, and finally isolated it. The Divine then spoke to this man's knowledge. If Doctor Salk had sat down somewhere, or wandered around and wielded a magic wand, or had taken a vacation, it would not have come to him. One must combine one's physical and spiritual capabilities to achieve some purpose.

Some want achievement free, or by a shortcut. But the Divine Will does not function that way. There may be exceptions. But the quickest and most ordinary way is to discipline oneself. In India we call it yoga, which simply means to yoke oneself. To what? To Divine power. But how? We have the body, we have the mind, we have consciousness, we have self-consciousness, we have super-consciousness. We have to go to each level, because truth is multi-leveled. We cannot trigger the ultimate by simply taking a pill or doing some trick—like levitation and reaching up to the ceiling. Such things are trivialities.

Yoga begins by saying that any yogi who wants "supernatural" powers is tricking himself. We call it "Yoga-Samkat" (the crisis of a yogi) when someone wants to achieve something without employing the proper means. We have to acquire knowledge and control before we can achieve the wholeness of meaning. This is a delicate theme. How, then, do we "achieve" the wholeness of being? The main thing is to be what one is. In Thomas Merton's words, "Let us be that which we already are." It is already there, but we have to discover it. How do we discover it? That is the big thing! By discipline, by purity, by holiness, and by following the Absolute. Also there must be a rectitude in the passionate and persistent fulfillment of our task. This means we must be in harmony with the end we are seeking.

We cannot swim through rivers of blood into peace; we cannot lie our way into truth. But this is what we are trying to do—politicians especially. We take the exact opposite course and wish to reach our goal. Even when we are sincere, we will never do so. We plunge the world into another cycle of terrible suffering, misery, death, maiming, murder, as we have seen in our time, and it has happened again and again. But there are some who know how the ends connect, such as a Saint Francis of Assisi or a Buddha. They are conscious of the purity of means and the truthfulness of the ultimate end. In India, yoga insists on this, and the kind of suggestive power that is brought to bear in our contact with daily things is stupendous.

There is a passage in Thomas Merton's *Asian Journal* describing what Merton experienced in Sri Lanka. He was looking at one of the great statues, and found a living presence.

I have had a similar experience. I was walking in the forest in Bodh-Gaya, the site of Buddha's supreme enlightenment, when I saw a man completely absorbed in prayer. I could see him very clearly—the moonlight even at ten at night was so bright, one could have read a letter by it.

I said to myself, "I won't disturb this hermit." But he didn't move. Nothing moved. I became very curious, so I went up closer. It was a Buddhist *statue*, centuries old. But it was so alive—much more so than I was, much more so than the whole crowd of people around. The concentration, the luminosity it radiated, was both of passion and compassion. This figure was built on an image of the great master who taught us the whole meaning of compassion, which includes passion, but passion in the direction of kindliness, of beatitude, and of grace.

Thomas Merton experienced this in his own way. He wasn't expecting it. That is what made it very powerful. He speaks of the claims of "paganism" and all that—worshiping a tree, or a stone. But Merton is barefooted and undisturbed, fulfilled in the wet grass and the wet sand. He says: "Then, the silence of the extraordinary faces . . . the great smiles . . . huge and yet subtle. Filled with every possibility, questioning nothing, knowing everything, rejecting nothing; the peace, not of emotional resignation but of Madhyamika, of sunyata"—the middle path, the convergence which brings the truth.

Sunyata means emptying one's mind of what is non-essential. What seems to be empty is really not empty; it is like the sky which, though apparently empty, is filled with stars. There was a kind of pervasive stillness and wholeness that Merton felt about those statues, which established a profound meaning without refutation. There was no combativeness, no celebration. There were none of those acrobatics which very often go by the name of "mystical" Oriental religion. There was only a pure surrender to something so much greater than the self.

Merton continues: "I was knocked over with a rush of relief and thankfulness at the *obvious* clarity of the figures, the clarity and fluidity of shape and line, the design of the monumental bodies composed into the rock shape and landscape . . . And the sweep of bare rock sloping away on the other side of the hollow . . . Looking at these figures I was suddenly, almost forcibly, jerked clean out of the habitual half-tied vision of things, and an inner clearness,

clarity, as if exploding from the rocks themselves . . ."
All became evident and obvious, "the queer *evidence* of the
reclining figure, the smile," the smile of someone who has
attained an infinite joy.

This is the kind of realization Merton and the others
were seeking at the Temple of Understanding Conference
in India the week prior to his visit to Sri Lanka. This is
where all the world meets, all peoples, of all races, all
religions, without any barrier.

At the Vedanta Center in Cohasset, Massachusetts,
which is guided by the saintly lady, Srenata Gayathi Devi,
there is a way of observing the morning hour with prayer.
They begin by singing a chant, as in the monastery at
Gethsemani where Thomas Merton lived and worshiped.
It was my privilege to join in the chant at Gethsemani in
the early morning. The Vedic chants are sometimes almost
identical with the Catholic chants, especially the Gregorian.
Many of us do not get up at a very early hour, but some do.
They experience the dawn. Gradually the light grows. There
is a fresh flush of gold and blue. It's a beautiful hour. We
see the dawning of a new day, the blossoming of new power.

The evening hour is also celebrated at the Vedanta
Center, with some Vedic verses. They would seem like rank
pagan worship to some, honoring tree and rock and what-
not. But it is not that. "He who has given the fire, the air,
the earth, the trees, the medicine of the trees, the fruitage
of the earth (add a few more things) - to him let us bow in
salutation." This prayer is part of the ritual of acceptance
and thankfulness at Tagore's Santiniketan in India. They
are not saying "I worship this tree, I worship that rock,
I possess this particular symbol of the universe." Rather
they realize that deep within the very structure of the atom,
or the star, the infinitesimal as well as the infinitudinal,
there is the handiwork of the Divine. If we are so bereft of
spiritual power as to miss it in the created universe, we
might even miss it in our moments of beatitude, when we are
sequestered and concentrated, because we have not acti-
vated our conscience, our sense of beauty, our sense of the
Divine, through daily contacts. It requires very little else.

We can see this in the face of an old woman, weeding in the field. She looks up, and we see her face lined with compassion, with kindliness. A whole lifetime of service, of self-abnegation, has given this simple woman a spiritual beauty which the great artists will seek more than the gilded face of a cinema star. The whole of her life is written there, and when we see that, passing through a village, we have seen the face of God. That is strong language. But what is wrong with saying, "I have experienced him in that old grandmother"? She is nobody special . . . few people know her . . . her name is not in the papers. But she is there. Bent over a child or over her daily tasks, she is one who has achieved an inner maturity. India has always insisted on this. Though we are to select places and occasions, special spiritual hours and pilgrimages, the meaning of it all lies in our being enlightened, and enlightenment comes from such pure moments of contact.

This is very like Zen, only the whole quest is for truth itself. We don't leave out daily life. Neither does Zen. But there is spaciousness.

In Christianity there is service. We cannot separate devotion from service. If we do, devotion will be too abstract. If we have only service, as we sometimes do in our days—lots of gift packages given, especially by politicians who want to buy the good will of people by that kind of handout—it is terrible. It is tyranny! But if we are giving freely the whole of who we are—this is something which India has always prized.

Many of the peace marches with Gandhi had the quality of the experience we have been speaking about. On one occasion, when Gandhi was seventy-eight, he walked fifteen miles. The temperature was 110 in the shade, the hottest time of the day. It was really desperately difficult; and when he arrived at his destination, he found nothing. The village had been burned down by rival factions—the Hindus and Moslems—who had just gone on a kind of spree of self-destruction or suicide. As Gandhi said, "Every fratricide is an act of suicide." They had destroyed everything. As we stood there, dumbfounded, Gandhi said,

"There must be someone here!" We searched, and found three women, their veils drawn, standing near a row of coconut trees. This was in my area, in a sense. I'm a Bengali. I speak that language. Gandhi had acquired just a slight knowledge of it. So he said to me, "Ask them what we can do to help." They did not answer, but kept an unbroken silence. Again I asked, "Can we do anything? Gandhi is here." One of the women then said, "Ask Gandhi to go away." Gandhi said, "She may be right. But why?" She answered. "They took my child and threw it into the river."

What can one do for a person who is in such a state of mind? Could Gandhi give back a life? Could Gandhi give them some kind of wishful consolation? He said, "Tell her I have nothing to give. I'm not the government, I'm not the army, I'm not the police, I'm not the treasurer. I've come because I'm the elder brother. I have the right to share your suffering." Then he stretched out his hand—an empty hand. A gift packet would have been an insult and an anti-climax. But he had brought the whole of himself. And the eyes of those women dimmed. There was an immediate change. He had the right as an older man to be there, to bear witness. What more can one do sometimes but say: "God is here! I cannot relieve your pain, but I can bear witness to your suffering, and to the presence of the Divine Father." Gandhi didn't put it into words, but his message was unmistakable.

Then a change began to take place. One of the women said, "We feel so sad that we cannot give you anything. When guests come to our house or our village, we give them a banana or a coconut, or whatever. But now we have nothing to give." He said, "That's not your problem. We're all right. We'll go back fifteen miles to where we came from. We have plenty. But you have nothing." So you see, their normal desire to be hospitable, to be kind—which they were—returned, because he brought them that empty hand, those empty hands, and they were filled.

This is the kind of language that is universal. I don't think anyone would misunderstand. But generally it is the politician who comes before anyone has spoken to a people who have been hurt. The carriers of the virus of hatred, these political people, all kinds of men with special purposes, contaminate the people's minds. "We will take three more lives to compensate for the loss of your baby." What would that do for a mother? No mother would say, "I'll be satisfied if three more babies are killed." It would be hideous! They don't speak that way, unless such violence is put into their minds by newspapers, the radio, suggestive media, and the like. But whatever happens, India comes back to the person; the Divine comes to the community or the family, to the continued witness of those whose character is his framework.

If you saw Gandhi—he was not a photogenic person—he looked like an ordinary person, a grandfather in any village in India. But when you took a second look you suddenly discovered his character, built brick by brick, over many years; he had that frame of reference which is so unmistakable. That is what India has believed in. Sometimes they have followed the wrong leaders. But they believed in the divinity of man, and have also believed in the divinity of the things that man creates. Of course, he does not create of himself; everything he creates is initially a gift of God, whether it is of marble, or clay, or a musical instrument. The elements are all gifts; he has combined them in a new way and that is good.

If you do not have a musical instrument, you cannot become a Rachmaninoff or a Heifetz, or any of the great musicians. Yet they are themselves in their own technical way. They know there's music that is divine. When there is no divinity attached to the sound it is just sound. How can sound of itself tell us about the Spirit? When it does, we know the player is filled with the Divine Spirit. In music we strike that ultimate Divine in sound. But it is not enough for us to say that we are filled with the Spirit, and then sing a song or a chant. The chant, in order to be meaningful, depends on a trained voice, as well as a trained person with character.

At Gethsemani, I sometimes rose at night to join the procession of monks who were going upstairs to sing the Gregorian chant. At such times there was an illumination of the Spirit, such as India believes in. We have to provide an occasion for it, we have to create the circumstances, the atmosphere. And then, whatever is there—the dawn, red and gold, the evening star shining above, or the rain-bearing clouds darkening the horizon—all seems to come together in what Thomas Merton called *constantia*. That is a very good word. Every single note of life is a distinctive note. But when we play these notes, something is built up that is irreversible, indestructible. That is the constant thing—very mystical, very profound; mystical in the right sense. So we have to train, we have to be in tune, we have to learn.

Many in our time want a pill to do it or they want a guru to do it for them. They want to get there cheap, but they never arrive. They think they have, but how can you learn to play a piano without five-finger exercises? I admit I have great sympathy and love and respect for many of the hippies who are my students, but they want a shortcut. They say, "We got it!" because they went into the woods and were riding high. (I didn't ask whether they took some kind of pill, or whatever.) "We felt we were really writing better than Shakespeare, composing better than Beethoven." I didn't refute them. I asked: "Did you drive back home after you had this supreme experience?" "We couldn't drive; all our limbs were shaking." I wanted to ask, "How could you write like Shakespeare if you couldn't hold a pen in your hand? Or how could you play the piano if your hands were in such a condition?" Instead, I said: 'Well, did you have a good appetite, a sense of well-being?" They were sick!—in a pathological condition! A powerful drug, an LSD, can sometimes remove a road-block under the guidance of a great doctor, but not in the hands of a young person who knows nothing about the potential of even a tiny globule of LSD or other drugs. They don't have the right knowledge; they don't know what they are pursuing. They want an instant miracle, but they will never get it. This is pitiful, because their purpose is true. The young people are searching as much as any older spiritual person, but many of them have missed the mark.

In yoga we touch the main line of India. It is strenuous

and arduous, but we do not make an acrobatic display of sheer control for its own sake. We don't go in for that. But we do go in for what is relevant, like breath control. I once asked the late Dr. Paul Dudley White, one of the greatest heart specialists of our century, how at eighty he was able to bicycle around Boston. He replied that exercise never hurts our heart; it is because we don't know how to keep the rhythm of our body, which depends much on our breathing, that we deteriorate. I said, "You are saying what they said about yoga!" He asked: "What did they say?" I replied: "That a few minutes of rhythmic breathing will give you a sense of composure." He answered: "If you make a fetish of it, it won't make you a Beethoven or a Saint Francis. But a reasonable practice will make you more harmonious. The heart has a certain maximum and minimum in its intake and emission of oxygen. If we learn how to regulate that process just a little we will be the gainer. I see young people going up stairs, panting for breath. That is not the way to do it. We can climb a hundred stairs, but we must pause a bit while we are going up, and see that our heart is not fluttering, that we are not over-taxing our resources." That's all there is to it!

Do what you do harmoniously. The sages learned through mistakes and hard experience. One can make a display of poverty—just as wealth is displayed. Yoga says, follow the middle way. We need food for our body. Food is divine, and the body is divine, too, on its own level. If we feed the body properly, moderately, we will be fit. The instrument is ready to be played by the master's hand. If we are unready, if the string is too slack, or too taut, it will not produce music. We have to know how to tune our instrument; that is part of yoga. Where training is concerned there are many basic rules. We don't know all of them, but this is one that is basic. There is the body; it is the foundation, in a way, of all life. Then there is the mind. We cannot have mental freedom simply by wishing for it.

Very often our state is like that of a chariot being drawn by fifty horses in fifty different directions. We will never reach our destination if we ride in that kind of a vehicle.

But if we have two horses, going in one direction—single-pointed—we will get there. We must control our mind, not to the extent of paralyzing it, but making it resilient and giving it a sense of direction. This requires thought. It requires daily discipline, sometimes just sitting still. However, meditative discipline is being capitalized and exploited in our time. Ten minutes, fifteen minutes, and anyone can gain sublimation, whether a black-marketeer or a man who has burned down a village! This is not so, of course, because we must create conditions that are favorable for nurturing the element that is within us. The masters tell us: "Be still, like a jar of water." The silt sinks to the bottom and the water becomes more and more clear. This is not something we can practice at a moment's notice, but it contains a basic truth. "Be still!"

Sometimes when we think a man is being very active, he is very passive. Many of the movements that we indulge in are inertial movements, not innovative, not energetic. This is true of most of the hectic things that people do. I think of Clive Street in Calcutta or Wall Street in New York. People there can't be still for five minutes. They have armies of secretaries and dozens of phones. If they are alone in a room they face a vacuum. In my travels I met such a person, and he said to me: "For all I care, I could blow out my brains." I asked why. He thought he would get a bit of yoga from a supposedly knowledgeable Hindu (which I am not). So I asked him: "What's wrong?" "Oh." he said, "I have houses in Florida, I have apartments in New York, I have a formidable bank account, I even have a very fine family. But I get nothing out of it all. I could blow out my brains!" I said, "This is something you can solve by changing the basic rhythm of your life. You can and must slow down, by making space, by confronting yourself, and by confronting other people's problems. It is not just you in a vacuum, opting for a limitless emptiness. That is not how it happens."

As Buddha said, "I cannot reach the ultimate unless I take others with me." Convinced that we are not alone, he waited for the lost one and the least one. There is the whole illumination of consciousness. There are would-be

Buddhas in all cultures. They are potential Buddhas in the sense of being potential divine beings who have neglected themselves.

Buddha said: "Calm yourself, have a sense of compassion, and start on the road." Then he prescribed twelve good disciplines and the eightfold noble path. People say he ended in Nirvana, nothing less. If we want to enter nothingness, we don't have to pursue an eightfold noble path. We can just fall into a well or jump into the ocean. But that's not it. Buddha began with right conduct, right direction, right control, and right-mindedness. With these one begins to realize the meaning of Nirvana. It is transcendence, not extinction.

Let us not separate the aesthetic, the intellectual, the spiritual, and the higher religious experiences. I believe they belong together. They are not separated by dividing walls. Sometimes an aesthetic impulse can release a higher impulse; sometimes spiritual illumination will make a better artist. We appropriate to ourselves a knowledge which we do not natively possess. When we go to India or to any hard-working rural community we are humbled by the sight of infinitely patient men and women doing their daily work. It is sad that they are so often exploited. When they are left to themselves, taking a boat out on the river or singing a song under a banyan tree, they spontaneously begin to compose songs.

Illiterate persons have picked up wisdom from the lore of traditions, from the kindliness of their people. Spirituality is a pervasive quality. It is ignited by art; it is triggered by processes of discipline, by meditation, which allows one to be single-minded, to let the dust settle and the water become clear. This is what counts above all: the gradual clarification of our sense of the divine. When we reach this stage, we are a whole person.

One day when I was at an interfaith conference in Calcutta (Thomas Merton and I were in the same hotel), I stepped out into the street in front of the hotel and saw Merton standing there, gazing at the people walking and driving by. I asked what he was looking at. He answered, "Everything!" And he meant just that: clouds in the sky, cows running loose in the street, rich men, beggars—a colorful procession. He was taking it all in. I don't know what his impressions were; there were a lot of things that needed to be remedied. But they couldn't be remedied by gunpowder or empire-building or any such power; only through understanding, through greater love. And Merton had that. People at that meeting would look at his face and ask, "Who is this American saint?" None of us had said that he was a saint, but they saw it in his face.

One day I asked Merton: "Would you like to visit an artist, a very remarkable man who is in his eighties? He is a master artist." He answered, "I have an hour and a half; will that be enough?" I said yes, so we went in a friend's car to the artist's house. The artist didn't know much English, but he looked what he was. He had a very beautiful face. He was a genuine artist. He said: "Tell this American saint that what I really do is part of the whole. I make my colors from original seed, clay and chemicals. I make my brush; I make my paper. This is my vocation; this is my livelihood; this is also my worship."

Thomas Merton replied, "That is exactly what we do in the monastery. Tell our friend this: A man does not change. When I bake bread, I want it to be good bread. When I till the ground, it has to be a straight furrow. When I make cheese, it must be good cheese. If I sing Gregorian chant, I must take the right tone. If I pray, as a result of all these actions and more, it must be deep prayer. Wholeness is what we have preserved." I related all this to the artist and his face shone with joy.

As we went from one room to another, we saw many kinds of paintings. The artist had never gone outside his own city, not to speak of going outside of India. He really knew nothing about doctrinal or traditional Christianity. But he knew people, he knew places, he knew the world. There were some pictures of Jesus, including a Crucifixion, on one of the walls. Thomas Merton stopped at one of them; he was entranced.

I said to him: "You know, monks are not supposed to

carry big money-bags. Suppose someone buys that picture for you, where would you like it to be delivered?" "Gethsemani," he answered, and added: "That's a good place." Naturally, for that was his place. "But," he added after a moment, "I think there could be another place ... Our Lady of the Redwoods, in California." It was from there he had taken off on this his last journey. As you know, he never returned, for he was killed by an electric shock. He had mentioned some other name. When I returned to the hotel I found a note: "Her name is Mother Myriam. She is in the Redwoods Abbey. It is not far from San Francisco. This is her telephone number."

I bought that painting; soon afterward Merton died. I was so stunned that for almost a year I didn't take any steps to contact Redwoods Abbey. Then when I found I was going to be near San Francisco, I put in a phone call. Mother Myriam answered. I began to say "I have a special ..." but she interrupted me and said: "You don't have to tell me. I already know about it. I'm expecting you." I asked how I could reach her. She answered: "That's not your problem —it's ours. Tell me when you'll be at the San Francisco airport." When I arrived at the airport at 8 P.M. there was a monk waiting for me with a car. I thought the abbey was just around the corner ... It was a four-hour drive! Who does things like that, and why?

When I reached that monastery I experienced its sanctity not only in the beautiful community of twelve or thirteen nuns, living there a very solitary life, but also in the tall pines which may have been there when Jesus walked this earth. Those great redwood trees and the Pacific Ocean, blue and expansive—the whole of it became a composition of great beauty, sublimity and prayer. We decided not to do anything that evening; in the morning we would start to share.

Those holy nuns were profoundly moved by the picture of Jesus. The artist had put into it a kind of intense blue and gold. There is not a drop of blood anywhere, because the truth is, Jesus triumphed. They said it was rather like early Syriac paintings. Being innocent of any knowledge of such paintings, how did the Hindu artist get this view? If you have a pure mind, when you meditate on the Beatitudes or read the Sermon on the Mount, your belonging to a different tradition does not exclude you from penetrating into their deeper meanings. It might conceivably even give you some special insights.

I want to emphasize this: a man who has been raised in the atmosphere of growing corn, of children playing on the ground, of honest men and women toiling for their daily bread, may share a wholeness, a rightness, which makes him ready for the kind of experience that goes to a still higher state. I believe the religious state is such.

As you know from Zen, we can take off at any point. It is almost as if it were without preparation, but in reality there is a lot of preparation. A great Zen philosopher, Suzuki, was perhaps the foremost exponent of one type of Zen. He always insisted on the exercises of the different traditions. Toward the end of his life he wrote a book on the disciplines of the monastery. Some have thought that all that is needed is to see two birds fly away, and you've got it. Well, that is so; but in seeing those birds fly, you are putting something into your experience. You suddenly see two little birds, which have no compass, no map, daring the evening sky and the clouds and finding their way through it all; it is a kind of visible miracle.

A very famous Zen monk heard of a still greater man— an older person. In order to know the Supreme Truth he went to him and said, "I want to know the meaning of it all, of life." The old man shook his head but said nothing. The monk had been reading, not the book of life, but the printed books of discipline, so he had to bring him to the Book itself. However, he simply said, "Do you see that stream? It is shallow, you can cross it. What do you see beyond it? A clump of trees. Why don't you go there?" He was saying this to a monk who was seeking the meaning of "Life." Why should the monk cross that little stream and go to the clump of trees? Because the master had told him to: that's all. So he went. When he entered that little forest-like place he saw many woodcutters at work, their muscles rippling in the sun—hard work, an honest man's work—and the whole situation took on meaning: through work, through association, through people, through concern, we understand life; not by isolating ourselves and thinking we have a monopoly on God because we are doing something very specific. We can do that, but not at the expense of the contact which brings us in touch with the holy dust of the world, the beautiful flowers that bloom in the garden, of children's faces, of a mother bending over her sick child. These are the witnesses of the Divine. An Indian saint does not by-pass these. I think somehow the charisma has been lost. The people have lost the trail from time to time. But, like Zen, it was kept up in the monasteries. The monks so disciplined themselves, they hardly ever committed faults.

One of Suzuki's disciples wrote a book called *The Flower Does Not Speak*. He left his book on Suzuki's desk, during the last ten days or so of the master's life. He never thought that Suzuki would be able to do anything with it, but later, after the master had died, they found that he had written an introduction to the little book, in English. One of the most amazing things Suzuki said in his introduction was: "A flower becomes a flower. The moon saunters in the ultimate sky and shines. Why should God give it speech? He doesn't have to. The whole meaning of a flower is to be a flower. The whole meaning of the moon is to shine. What is the whole meaning of man? To be human." As Tagore said, the hardest thing for a man is to be human. It doesn't come automatically, like a bird growing wings. It comes out of discipline, out of what in India they speak of as "being twice born." It comes about by breaking through the shell of the ego, and emerging into our spiritual life. We share one life with all biological life; that is not too much. But we have to break through the shell of the ego, even as the birds do. If the little chick inside the shell stays comfortably within the shell, it will never know itself. It will die in the shell. But everything in the chick makes it peck away at the only protection it knows, which is the shell. Then it emerges into the limitless world of grass and blue sky.

Man has to do much more to emerge from his ego-shell. The masters give many, many suggestions as to how to do it. But when this is done and the ego is controlled, the higher discipline takes over. We are not asking for a miracle in the cheap sense. A true miracle is that which is happening all the time, but it is made to happen in a special sense when we have a deep concern; then somehow we acquire a higher power.

The deepest type of discipline is prayer, is holiness of life, and this is what Thomas Merton had. Before he spoke to the Dalai Lama, I asked: "Why do you want to see him? He's from a different tradition." Merton replied: "But prayer and silence! We Catholics have both and they have them too. They pursue them in the mountain remoteness. We are on the same wave-length." That's exactly what he said. And he found it to be so when he spoke with the Dalai Lama; there was that kind of communication.

I don't say that Catholic and Buddhist prayer and silence are identical. They couldn't be! I don't know much about Tibetan Buddhism, but from the little I know of it, it is very different from the sublimity of my whole religious experience; but there is an affinity. Merton immediately discovered this, and the Dalai Lama said, "You are already a liberated being, in the Buddhist sense."

We have pursued these values in the East, not with a view to mastering some kind of miraculous power, but because we are drawing from the deepest and the greatest legacy of human experience. As I said in the beginning of this paper, the adventure of man on this planet is one; a single Divine Life has been implanted in each of us, whether we are in Africa, or New Zealand or anywhere else. Just a few weeks ago I went to the fabulous South Sea Islands, and I was astounded at the power and the beauty of those simple people on some of those small islands, such as Tahiti or Samoa. Great artists and great writers went there and found what they sought. I especially recalled Robert Louis Stevenson's discovery of Samoa. On arriving on that island I sought his grave, which is on a hill. The laborious climb was almost too much for me. With the help of a few of the local boys I found the slab of stone, on which was carved the well-known poem he had written long ago. He did not mean it to be an epitaph for his grave, but it was found suitable by his friends on the islands:

> Under the wide and starry sky,
> Dig the grave and let me lie.
> Glad did I live and gladly die,
> And I laid me down with a will.
> This be the verse you grave for me:
> 'Here he lies where he longed to be;
> Home is the sailor, home from the sea,
> And the hunter home from the hill.'

Robert Louis Stevenson arrived *home* on a distant island in the South Pacific. How did he feel about this? And how did the simple villagers feel who knew nothing about the great Scottish writer who wielded a kind of magic pen and yet felt he was one of them? There was a kind of genuine mingling, a coming together of people. We are discovering this now in Japan; we are discovering it in Tibet; we are discovering it among ourselves. India and Europe and America have been in touch with each other for ages, centuries. We have only to remove the barriers that have been created by false experts; then things will flow again.

If religion is not relational it is not religion. If it separates us, there is something wrong. So let us come back to that relational spirit which was so evident in what Thomas Merton and others like him have done. Let us affirm the call of the Divine unity in the human being. If we do not experience it in another human person, be he black or brown or yellow or green,—we have to change the colors sometimes—we will never find God.

I would end by saying—this may sound very controversial but I hope it is not—that the whole nature of God, though it has been manifested through revelation, is still being manifested. We have not heard the last thing about God; creation is still going on, and God is here. So if we have left the present in pursuit of solid and solidified texts which contain the ultimate forever, we have somewhere missed the living presence of the Divine, who wants us to discover anew the meaning of his existence and the meaning of each others' existence through the links that are provided by the relational power of religion.

2

THOMAS MERTON, NOW AT THE CRACK OF DAWN

David Steindl-Rast, O.S.B.

There is danger of speaking too much about Thomas Merton and too little about his deep concerns. We should be aware of that danger and make special efforts not to fall into hero worship in speaking of him. Rather, we should dwell upon the things he stood for. He still stands for them because he is more alive in the minds of people today than he was before he died. One of the most important things Merton advocates is the marginal man taking a stand against labels. If we follow this carefully, we may find that we arrive at our own center by the guidance of Thomas Merton, precisely because we choose to be marginal.

One of the most dangerous labels is the label of "contemplation," of "contemplative." If there was one thing that Merton was always stressing, it was: "Don't label me. Don't call me a hermit. If I allow you to call me a hermit I will have to live up to your expectation of what a hermit ought to be like. Don't call me a monk; you have your idea of what a monk is. I might or might not conform with that idea. I'm just myself."

I think the whole life of Thomas Merton could be summed up as one long case of Merton *versus* labels. That is what he was all about—knocking down one label after another, and, of course, constantly identifying himself again in one way or other. The moment he discovered this was a label, he ruled it out.

Yet the whole idea of labels isn't as simple as that. It is a complex thing, especially in the context of monastic life, and very complex in the context of Benedictine monastic life. One of the words that comes up over and over again in the Rule of Saint Benedict, according to which Merton lived half his life, is what the different things, places, and offices in the monastery are to be: "*sit quod dicitur*—let it be what it is called, let it come up to its name." The abbot: "Let the abbot be what he is called." The oratory: "Let the oratory be what it is called." So there is a real thrust in the Rule of Saint Benedict to take things and words and ask, "What is it to be called? Is it *really* what we call it? It ought to be what it is called. Let it come up to its standard." And a name sets a standard.

This is profoundly biblical because in our biblical tradition a name is much more than a label. The name is the very essence of the thing, and for a thing or a person to be true means to live up to the name. God is faithful to his name. The people ought to be what they are called; that is, a royal priesthood. There is a very fine line between labels and being what one is called. Maybe the clue to the solution of this problem in the context of monastic life is given when we look at the very name and "label" of the monk. One could almost say that to be a monk means to be one without labels. So the label of monk or name of monk is to designate one who has no label, who constantly strives to outgrow labels. That is the one vocation of the monk.

To look at it from a different point of view, the very name *monachos* has been translated, understood, or explained in the course of tradition, both in the label sense and in the counter-label sense. In the label sense, as being "one who lives alone." *Monachos* means the "loner," and unless you live alone, you are not really a monk. Hence, an external label. If you don't come up to that label, you are not really a monk. Various other aspects of being a *monachos* suggest that it is always an external thing; that is has something to do with being "one." The monk is the one-joy man who goes after one thing; the single-minded man pursuing one purpose.

From another point of view, monastic tradition has interpreted the term *monachos* from within rather than from without, and not so much as a label. The *one* is a goal rather than a frame of reference. The monk is the one who strives to "one" himself or herself, the one who goes toward integration. Monastic life is precisely the constant effort to overcome labels by becoming unique. Merton upheld that as a special gripe, or goal if you will, for himself. It was a gripe when he was chafing against the bit, and a goal when he was speaking freely: "Make room in the monastery for idiosyncrasies! This is a place for crackpots. This is a place for misfits. If you aren't misfit everywhere else, there is no room for you in the monastery. Give elbow-space especially for uniqueness." Not uniqueness as another label—"Let's all try to be *unique*"—but by just being yourself. Become *yourself*, the one you are called to be. That's the very unpretentious self, called to become an integrated person, the truly integral self.

Counter-culture has coined an expression that fortunately has now become part of everyone's vocabulary, and expresses that point well. When we speak of a person who is really the way one ought to be, an integrated person, we say that person is *together*. The word "together" fits perfectly into this context and expresses well what it means to be a monk. What one strives for in monastic life is to be "together." You aren't saying "together *with*" this or that; just *together*. You leave this together open, to being applied to everything. Together with himself or herself, together with all others, with everyone and everything, together with the cosmos, together with God, together with ultimate reality, just together. To be in this sense "together" is what it means to be unique. A person who is really together has transcended labels by finding the place where all labels apply or none.

To be really *together* means to find what tradition calls the "place of the heart." The heart is the "together" place.

When a person finds his or her heart and lives from the heart, that person is together. The heart is that realm where we are completely together. There we are together with ourselves, because the heart is the taproot, so to say, of the whole person, where we are not divided into intellect and will and emotion, into body and mind, but are one with ourselves.

In our heart we are together also with all others because when we really find the center of our being, we are truly "alone" in the sense of being all-one and so one with all. When you find your heart, you have found that place where you are not only most intimately by yourself, but most intimately united with all others. That is the paradox, the mystery of the heart. And in the heart I am also most intimately together with God, because at my very center God is closer to me than I am to myself, as St. Augustine says. The heart is where I find God. You could look at the whole monastic quest as a quest for finding the heart, and living from the heart. But this is also, in a sense, the quest of every Christian, the quest of every human being.

In order to become truly human you have to live from the heart. We are all concerned with one goal in the spiritual life: to find the heart and to live from the heart. But in monastic profession one makes a "profession" of this. Thus the monk is, so to say, a professional in quest of living from the heart. This is not a boastful statement. We all know that nowadays professionals are often not better than others at what they profess to know or do. They only charge a lot. Often we prefer amateurs to professionals because they do it with love, as the name "amateur" says, while the professional simply does it for a living. Thus, monastic profession implies responsibility. By making profession, one takes upon oneself a specific responsibility. If you are a doctor by profession, you have a responsibility, and it can entail legal inconvenience if you don't live up to what you profess. If you make monastic profession, I don't think anyone would take you to court for not living up to your profession, but it does have no less real implications. You are expected to be engaged in that pursuit, that quest of the heart. All human beings are engaged in this quest in the context of their spiritual life, but the monk is professionally so.

When we speak about someone like Thomas Merton, who in our time exemplified for many thousands and maybe hundreds of thousands of people what it means to be a monk, we are really speaking about something which is of extreme importance to every one of us, because we are speaking about a person who struggled to live up professionally to something which most of us do as amateurs. Now this is something which all of us ought to do as perfectly as we can, namely, find the heart and live from the heart. That simply means life in fullness. As Jesus said, "I have come that they may have life, and have it more abundantly."

The heart stands for life. It is the organ that symbolizes for us the center of life. When the heartbeat stops, life stops. Life, especially under the image of the heart, is a pulsating reality; it is a give and take. Life in its most primitive form is seen by us in biology the moment we find an inside and an outside. Before that, we cannot speak of life. But the moment we have a semi-permeable membrane that lets in liquid and retains it, we have an inside and an outside, and we have the beginning of life. In all forms, from the most complex and spiritual forms of life to the simplest, this is one aspect that is never lost and never can be lost, that somehow there is an inside and an outside and some pulsating interaction, some give and take between the inside and the outside. This is beautifully expressed in the heart. Wherever there is life, we have an ingathering and an outgoing, a contraction and an expansion, a breathing in and a breathing out, a receiving of impressions and an expression of oneself. On all levels we have an embodying of some reality which is an inner reality. This is the point where contemplation comes in.

The very term "contemplation" (*contemplatio*) comes from the Latin and has its roots in Roman religion. *Contemplatio* has in its linguistic root the syllable *temp*. We still have this syllable in many English words: temperature, temperament, template (which a bricklayer uses for a particular pattern of arranging bricks or tiles), even tempest. When you look closely you find that words with this "temp" in both Latin and English, always have something to do with measurement. You measure temperature. The temples are supposed to be the measure of your height and breadth. The template is a measure according to which you lay out a pattern. So too the word temple. A temple was originally a measured area in the sky. The augurers, the Roman priests, measured out a certain area in the sky, and watched this area for the flight of birds. It was very important to see whether they flew from left to right or from right to left, from east to west, or some other direction, what kind of birds they were, and so on. But the decisive thing was that you watched an area in the sky, not on the ground below. The sky, filled with stars in perfect order, was contrasted to the earth, which was thought of as a rather disorderly and chaotic place.

From watching something up there in the sky-realm of order, you then project what happens up there down onto the earth. Order is projected down into chaos. Then an area of the ground that corresponds to that imaginary measured area in the sky is called the *templum*, and it is measured out by driving stakes and setting up stones, sometimes very heavy, very huge stones that cannot be moved, so that the immovable order in the sky is immovably projected onto the earth.

Now we are coming to a concept which far transcends the narrow limits of Roman religion, something absolutely basic to early human religiosity. We are immediately reminded of Stonehenge, for instance; there we find enormous boulders, and no one knows how they were moved into place. They are all set up to reflect the order of the sky. If, at the time of the equinox, we look between two boulders, we see a particular star rise in exactly that little slot. All at once we recognize that a gigantic sundial or stardial has been set up here.

Again, the *templum* was originally something in the sky, and then projected down onto the earth to reflect an order that is taken from somewhere else. We are looking at the eternal order projected down into the chaos of our everyday living. *Contemplatio*, then, is bringing together two temples: the eternal immovable measure in the sky, and its model in the midst of chaos down on earth. This understanding of *contemplatio* is ancient, and is found in Hindu and Roman and Celtic sacred traditions. But it is also familiar to us from our biblical tradition.

The great contemplative in the Bible is Moses. He is called by God up into the cloud, the cloud of unknowing. Forty days and forty nights Moses is with God on the high mountain, in the clouds. Then he comes down, and there follow those long, long passages (which we normally don't read, but we know they are there) in which the sanctuary is described. God had said to Moses on the mountain: "Build me a sanctuary . . . you must follow exactly the pattern I shall show you." The description goes into great detail regarding the tent and its coverings, its hooks and frames, its crossbars, its posts and its sockets. Every measurement is given in cubits and half-cubits. Every loop and ring and clasp of the tent sheets is counted. Every talent and shekel of gold, silver, and bronze is accounted for. Why all this? The decisive point is repeated after each section of the description. "And Moses built everything exactly according to the pattern that was shown him on the mountain." This whole elaborate process is gone through in order to bring home to us that we are to look up and project down. That we are to build, down here, everything just exactly as it was shown above on the mountain. "On earth as it is in heaven." This is how the Kingdom comes through contemplation.

It is easy to think of contemplation as the process of going up into the clouds, but that is only half of contemplation. *Contemplatio* means "on earth as it is in heaven." Bring the thing down! Unless you go up, you will not have the pattern according to which to shape the world down below. But if you just stay up there, you will not truly contemplate; you will just "template," or whatever, with your head in the clouds. You won't bring the Kingdom down. Therefore, Jesus spends the night on the mountain alone, in the desert alone, praying; but then He comes down into the crowd, and He is down here among us—very much so! He can afford to be so involved and dedicated to what He is doing here in the valley because He has this counter-balance of being able to go away and immerse Himself in complete exposure to the presence of God, alone on the mountain.

Thomas Merton was one of the pioneer contemplatives of our time. He discovered for himself that contemplation has two aspects; that contemplation is not only being up on the mountain, but it is also concerned with bringing the vision of the Presence of God down into daily life. I'm not too sure how soon he himself discovered how new all this was. It is so new because it is so traditional! If you are really traditional and involved with the roots of things, you are always in the forefront. I don't know how soon he himself discovered this, or how explicitly he discovered it, but it certainly took a very long time for others to discover it, particularly long for contemplatives. Contemplatives run a high risk of being stuck in one or other notion of what it means to be a contemplative. We are all prone to get stuck with labels. The decisive thing is that Merton broke out of these labels and blazed a trail for all of us.

In the monastic context, this *contemplatio*, this bringing together of the two temples, is expressed in creating the monastic environment. "Contemplative" is much, much broader than "monastic." One can be a contemplative without being monastic. Monasticism is a particular form of being contemplative. "Monastic" doesn't even refer to a lifestyle so much as it refers to an environment. "Monastic" is an adjective which primarily refers to an environment, an environment that is shaped by contemplation, and which in turn facilitates contemplation. So a monastery is a place, a professional environment, in which everything is geared toward facilitating that looking into the eternal order. Space and time are shaped by the rhythm of the seasons, the rhythm of the hours: something happens in the morning, at sunrise, that cannot be repeated. You cannot say, "My schedule calls for morning prayer at 7 o'clock or at 4 o'clock." One will seem more impressive than the other. But the real contemplative will not be impressed because you have your morning prayer at 4. The decisive thing about it is that your morning prayer will be when it is morning! Whenever it is morning on a given day, that's the time for your morning prayer. There is an objective element to be considered. When the sun rises, something actually happens. That is why, according to the Rule of St. Benedict, the schedule changes every day, as the morning prayer is adjusted to sunrise. Every day, when the sun rises, something unique happens. All the animals know it. The birds start singing. Even the monkeys, I understand, go up into the trees and celebrate Lauds up there!

I see Merton as a prophetic watchman for a new dawn in monastic and contemplative life. That is why he is so exciting for us. If he were simply a spokesman for something that had been going on for a long time and continues to go on, it wouldn't be so exciting. There is the expression: "the crack of dawn." Merton belongs to this "crack of dawn." When we were children, we would be so excited waiting for the moment when the chick would emerge from the shell, after pecking at it from the inside of the egg. When I saw the film of Merton's last talk at Bangkok I was reminded of this. It was like the "cracking-open" of the contemplative life, of monastic life, from the inside. There was something happening there. It was a very exciting talk and a very exciting picture, in spite of the fact that it really wasn't a very good address. Merton was never particularly good at giving public talks. He was best at personal conversations and informal breezy talks to small groups, like his students at Gethsemani. There is something very stange about this talk on Marxism and monastic life. Its interest lies precisely in the fact that Merton was speaking as a prophet almost in spite of himself.

In the Bible we have the story of the Prophet Balaam, who was invited by Balak, King of Moab, to *curse* the Israelites. Balak wanted him to stand up on a hill overlooking the Israelite camp in order to curse them. But on his way to the king, the ass on which Balaam was riding saw an angel blocking the way. The prophet didn't see the angel, but to his great embarrassment, the ass evidently did. Balaam's ass didn't want to go on; he squeezed Balaam's leg against the rock, trying to evade the angel as he passed down the road. Only by promising to say what the angel prompted him to say does Balaam get by. Finally, when he gets to the camp and tries to curse the Israelites, out comes a beautiful Advent prophecy about the star that is rising in Israel. The king who has called the prophet gets very angry and says: "Try again. Say something else." He tries again, and an even more glorious prophecy escapes his lips. Balaam says, "I can't say anything against the Lord. I have to say what the Lord wants me to say."

In the last talk Merton gave, at Bangkok, he is trying to talk about Marxism and the monastic life. We see in the film that he has notes before him. Consulting these notes in the Merton archives, we find only a few points of contact between them and the actual talk he gave. We also see that he was completely carried away. He goes on, a couple of times, and then comes back to his notes, but he keeps getting side-tracked. One almost has a feeling that there is some sort of a whirlwind or a current that draws him in another direction. He keeps hanging on to his notes, but gets dragged in another direction. He keeps talking about the monastery identity crisis (in the notes), but in the talk, in the very first paragraph, he has this interesting remark: "My purpose is perhaps to share with you the kind of thing a monk goes through in his, shall we say, identity crisis?" That is the word. So he is caught off guard, and starts talking about the identity crisis. Every single word here is significant: the "perhaps," the "kind of thing," the "vagueness" "the monk goes through," the whole idea of the transitus, the passage, the going through. And he is saying this just a few hours or minutes before his own going through the great *transitus*, his final passage, his—shall we say?—"identity crisis."

Again and again, he keeps coming back to this identity crisis, and that's what makes his talk so exciting. Merton himself says, "I am not an expert on Marxism, and what I have to tell you about this would be rather inconclusive." So it is not the formally announced topic that is exciting, but the dynamic prophetic undercurrent. Even as he goes on, you can tell from the way he is speaking that he feels the tug more and more. Then he switches from Marxism, leaving the topic completely behind, and in the second half of the talk he speaks only about Buddhism and Christian monasticism; so he has, in fact, abandoned his original track completely. Yet something comes through strongly and clearly: a confrontation with crisis, monastic identity crisis.

The very word "crisis" is connected linguistically with the words "sief" and "sifting." There is a connection between "sifting out" and "crisis" in the roots of these words. A crisis is a situation in which we sift things out. What is sifted out in an identity crisis is the question: "What are the essentials?" In speaking of the identity crisis, Merton struggled with the question, "What are the essentials of monastic life?"—sifting out the essentials. If you just go through the text of his Bangkok talk, underlining the words "essential" and "essentials," you will see at a glance Merton's main concern: "What are really the essentials?" The confrontation with Marxism simply provides the forum for confronting our own monastic life.

Merton says that the confrontation with Marxism forces him to face what it is to be a Christian monk. He tells a little story about meeting a Marxist student at California's Center for the Study of Democratic Institutions. During a break-period conversation, the student said to him, "We are also monks." It really sounded like: "We are the real monks! Who are you? We are the real dedicated ones." What is essential is that the monk take a critical attitude toward the world. The monk is a critic. We know from Merton's life to what extent he was a critic of our times. The monk has this in common with the Marxist, that both Marxist thought and monastic tradition are critical of society. But Merton says, Marxism criticizes and tries to change the economic structure; monasticism criticizes and tries to change man's consciousness. While Marxism is concerned with externals, monastic criticism is concerned with the inner attitude.

Merton sees a complete parallel between the movement in Marxist ideology from capitalistic greed to communist dedication, and, in monastic spiritual psychology, from selfish *cupiditas* to *caritas*, from selfishness and desire to real giving love. He calls that movement a great "yes" to reality, to love, the giving of oneself to life, to the other in service, rather than clinging and hanging onto and grasping. Unselfishness is one of the essentials which Merton sees in confronting the monastic crisis. We are critics, not uncritically entering some sort of frame of reference and doing what has always been done, but also very much like those who are on the social forefront of what is happening in our times. Real monks live with great alertness, criticizing, sifting out what is essential, and changing life accordingly.

This focus on change leads Merton to see a second essential of monastic life—transformation. Marxism doesn't simply make a comparison between capitalist greed and communist dedication, but it implies a call for change. Thus, monks cannot sit back and compare selfishness with love and service; there has to be a change taking place. It is a dynamic thing. Merton sees this liberation as a process, and monastic life as a *process* rather than a state of life. We have here one of those indications of a crack in the egg shell. Before Merton's time, monastic life was considered, on the whole, as a state of life. After Merton, this is no longer possible. It is a *process*. Of course, traditionally, this was always the ideal. Merton is very traditional in the true sense that to be *truly traditional* means to be on the forefront.

In the recent and customary view, but not necessarily the most deeply traditional one, monastic life was seen as a state into which one enters, a state in which one perseveres, rather than a process in which one goes forward dynamically to conquer new ground. Merton hinges this notion of progress and of transformation to what he calls the central monastic vow of *conversio morum, conversatio morum*. It is very interesting to note that he uses here the term *conversio morum*, translated as "conversion of life," which is one of the three Benedictine vows.

There has been a great controversy in the history of the Benedictine Monastic Order. Trappists included, whether Saint Benedict wrote: *conversio morum* or *conversatio morum*. *Conversio* is a conversion that takes place once and for all; *conversatio* is a conversion that is expressed over and over again. It does seem that even Saint Benedict's original text vacillated between *conversatio* and *conversio*. Our own monastic tradition emphasizes the fact that, regardless of what the original word was, we monks are to live in *conversatio*—in constant renewal and constant conversion, which is the very essence of monastic life. Merton, too, considers conversion as a constant turning to be of the very essence of monastic life. This is how he came to take a very critical attitude toward the structures of monastic life, and formulated this clearly when he said that the time for relying on structures has come to an end.

This may have become particularly clear to him through his visit with the Tibetans, which was the most important experience of his Asian Trip. His visit with the Dalai Lama and other Tibetan monks impressed Merton more than all other Asian encounters. Of course, these Tibetans have experienced Marxism as a force that destroyed much of their monastic structure. And Merton is confronting Marxism also as a political force that destroyed all structures. What happens when these structures are destroyed? In the future, he says, we will not rely on structures. We cannot be sure whether any of the structures with which we are familiar will outlast even our lifetime. What then are we supposed to do? What is the essence of monastic life?

Here is the high point of his whole Bangkok talk, the background of which is the story of Trungpa Rimpoche, who is now in the U.S.A., where he has founded a number of lively, prospering meditation centers. Merton met him on his Asian journey and was impressed. When the communists invaded Tibet, Trungpa Rimpoche was abbot of a large monastery, but was out on a visitation and got caught by the invasion at some farmhouse. Now the question was, what should he do? Should he go back to his own monastery or should he flee across the border? What should he do next? He sent a message to a nearby abbot-friend to ask, "What shall we do?" The abbot sent back a message which Merton found most significant: "From now on, Brother, everybody stands on his own feet."

Merton goes on to say, "To my mind, this is an extremely important monastic statement." (Remember, this man is now speaking in the last hours of his life!) "If you forget everything else that has been said, I would suggest that you remember this for the future: 'From now on, each one will have to stand on his own feet.'" He throws everything back on each monk personally: "Don't rely on structure; stand on your own feet." Then Merton expresses his relationship to structures: "Yes, we do need structures; we are supported by structures. But they may be destroyed at any moment by a political power or a political force. We cannot rely on structures. Use structures, but do not rely on structures."

The moment we stand on our own two feet, the moment we find contemplative life at the root of monastic life, deep down in our own hearts, in our own center, we go beyond division. That is the third essential that Merton sifts out in facing the monastic identity crisis: that the Christian monastic calling is one that unites us with all monks. There again is this crack where he breaks out from the enclosed shell of a Trappist, Christian, monastic structure into universal monasticism. Monks East and West share the same quest, the contemplative quest, the quest of the human heart, in which we are all united. We go beyond division to an inner liberty which no one can touch.

Merton sees the essence: "What is essential in the monastic life is not embedded in buildings, not in a habit, not necessarily even in a rule." (That must sound like enormous heresy to some.) "It is somewhere along the line of something deeper than a rule. It is concerned with this business of total inner transformation." Once we have reached that last inner quest for total inner transformation, to quote Saint Paul, "There is no longer slave or free-born, there is no longer Jew or Gentile," there is no longer Asian or European, but we have transcended these divisions. "This kind of monasticism," Merton said in his last talk, "this kind of monasticism cannot be extinguished. It is imperishable, it represents an instinct of the human heart."

Contemplative life in all its forms and on all different levels is really a quest for living from the heart. It is a quest *for* the heart. I would like now to go a little beyond the strict confines of Merton's talk in Bangkok, exploring something that here and there in his writings comes through which seems very important to me in the context, namely, the idea of the heart as the organ for finding *meaning*. The heart is the one center that unites us on the religious level with all human beings, everywhere in the world, at any time we engage in the ultimate quest for meaning. Just as with the eyes we perceive light, and with the ears we perceive sound, wherever we perceive meaning, it is with the heart. You can turn this around and say: by heart we mean the organ by which we perceive meaning. This is what heart means in the full biblical sense: it is that within us which responds to meaning. It is not only the intellect, although it must engage all of our intellect. It is not only the will, although all our devotion must enter into it. It is not only our emotions, although all our emotions must reverberate with it. It is the heart, that realm of our being where intellect, will and emotions are still one and united, the very taproot of our whole being.

Meaning is what really counts in our lives. If our life is filled to the brim with purpose, we may one day wake up and still wonder: Where is the meaning of it all? Purpose is not of itself meaningful. We must give meaning to our purpose; we must allow meaning to flow into our purpose, opening our hearts and giving ourselves to the Word of God, to the situation. There is more than purposefulness, and if we come to see it on many different levels, what really matters is not the useful but the superfluous! All the really great things in life, like poetry and music and friendship, are totally superfluous—superfluous in the sense of superfluity, of an overflowing, of not fulfilling any particular practical need, but being *gratis*. Then we come to see that the whole world is really superfluous. Who needs it?

We create the impression sometimes that God worked hard to make himself a world. Well, did he need it in the first place? No. It's a *superfluity of his love*; it's a superfluity of his enjoyment. It's not like someone making a woolen sweater against the cold, or a fan against the heat. No, it's much more like someone singing a song (in the shower, maybe, just for enjoyment). It is like someone dancing, an image that is often used in spiritual tradition—God as the Cosmic Dancer. Much more than work and purpose, all of creation is play, unfolding of meaning, celebration of the meaning that is at the root of it all.

This is where Merton's vision of the monk as the marginal man comes in: the monk at the margin of society, the monk as being totally superfluous. Nobody needs the monk, and yet, from another point of view, nobody needs anything as urgently as we need monks. For we need nothing more urgently than the superfluous. What would life be without poetry? What would life be without music? What would life be without friendship? But real friendship goes far beyond comradeship, where you still need one another. Comrades, like two sides of a step-ladder, hold one another up. But when you get to friendship, it is *pure gift*. It is more than practical help and support. It is mutual enjoyment. It implies this letting go, this freedom to let go. I am not bound to you. As the Sufis say, "Two birds tied to one another do not fly better for having four wings." That is something true friends understand. They fly with one another, but they are not tied to one another. They are completely free. The realm of our life where the superfluous matters most is our contemplative life. In that sense all of us have a contemplative life. The contemplative life of every human being consists in the search for meaning over and beyond purpose.

One of the theses that evolves from all of Merton's writings, but particularly from his Bangkok talk, is that the contemplative life is the secret in the heart of every human being. It belongs to all of us. It isn't the specialty of monks or anything like that. All of us are contemplatives. The second thesis flows directly out of that: If we are all contemplatives, and if the monastery is the controlled environment in which the contemplative life is professionally cultivated, a sort of laboratory—even Benedict called it a workshop—then everybody deserves life in a monastery, at least for a time.

That was another step where Merton cracked the egg of contemporary monastic life and went far beyond what his contemporaries could, or even now can, accept: that the monastery belongs to all. A monastery is not a kind of museum nor a place where you come and from a great distance look at the monks singing their chant down there, while you sit way up in the loft, removed from their life. Merton said, speaking about Trungpa Rimpoche again: "Incidentally"—for that's one of those incidental remarks where the real essence of the talk comes through—"incidentally, he has a monastery where you can be a monk for a time." "Incidentally," that is a possibility, and not only a possibility, it is a real need for our time. Everybody has, we all have, a contemplative life and so we all deserve monastic life.

Then he speaks about monastic therapy, a very ancient concept, monastic therapy, a healing that goes on in the monastery. God knows we all need that healing, and it isn't only for monks. The earliest monks in the West, the Essenes, were called "the Therapists." What this monastic therapy is all about is a liberation of the truth imprisoned in us by ignorance and error. It's not something outside, but it's an inner liberation, a liberation of the truth. Merton closes his talk with a very beautiful image. It is interesting that this image occurs in the original notes for the talk, but it occurs as a subheading somewhere in the middle of the talk. When a speaker takes something he has as a minor point and uses it as a final image, you can be sure that, either in the process of the talk or at some other point, this began to be very important to him. Here, an hour before he died, Merton uses an image from Buddhist iconography. The Buddha is seated, pointing toward the earth and holding a begging bowl.

The background of the story is that the tempter, immediately after Buddha's enlightenment, challenged him and said: "That little piece of ground on which you are sitting is really mine. You are sitting on my own little piece of ground." But the Buddha answered: "No, it now belongs to me because I have been enlightened." I belong to it, and it belongs to me. I belong to the world and the world belongs to me because I have been enlightened." Merton says, "This is a very excellent statement, I think, about the relation of the monk to the world. The monk belongs to the world, but the world belongs to him insofar as he has dedicated himself totally to liberation from it in order to liberate it."

We come now to a much deeper concept of *contemplatio*, which is liberation of the world. Buddha, holding the open begging bowl as a sign of total openness to everything given to him as a gift, points to the ground. Totally liberated, he can liberate the world, give himself to the world. That is the second half of *contemplatio*—putting the two temples together. Only when you are liberated can you liberate.

Merton says, "You can't just immerse yourself in the world and get carried away with it. That is no salvation. If you want to pull a drowning man out of the water, you have to have some support yourself. Suppose someone is drowning and you are standing on a rock, you can do it; or suppose you can support yourself by swimming, you can do it. There is nothing to be gained by simply jumping into the water and drowning with him." You must be liberated from the world to liberate the world. And that is the final word with which he leaves us at this talk. Liberation is the monastic life. It is imperishable, an instinct of the human heart.

That is the crack of dawn, that is the crack where I see Merton standing, just at the moment when he actually passes over into that life that is hidden with Christ in God. It is a crack that is widening these days.

The Lord is coming, the crack is widening.

The Lord can come in if we open up, and tremendous things are going to come from it.

3

THOMAS MERTON AND THE SEARCH FOR SOLITUDE

Richard Anthony Cashen, C.P.

I. The Challenge of Solitude

Thomas Merton, from the time of his entrance into religious life, felt a growing desire for more and more solitude. In his early days at Gethsemani Abbey, he struggled with the very real vocational question of whether or not the Trappists offered the kind of solitude and the amount of contemplation to which he felt he was called by God. He tried several times to transfer to the Carthusians and the Camaldolese. Eventually, he was allowed to live as a hermit as a Trappist at Gethsemani. But after only three years, he was searching for a more isolated spot to make his hermitage. Solitude was a driving passion in his life, because it was in solitude that he sought and found God.

It is not surprising, then, to find that solitude plays a large and important part in all his works. He wrote a lot about physical solitude. By physical solitude he always means—place, space, geographical separation from someone or something, a "getting away" or a "going apart." That was the kind of solitude he sought on entering the Trappists, and the greater solitude he longed for all during his religious life.

Important as physical solitude was to him and for him, interior solitude was even more important and more fundamental. He even said bluntly: "There is no true solitude except interior solitude."[1] Physical solitude may help foster inner solitude, it is true, but it is interior solitude which gives physical solitude its validity. Without true interior solitude, physical solitude might be a false or dangerous thing, full of self-hatred and life-denial, a flight from responsibility, or spiteful separation from one's fellow man.

For Merton, interior solitude is the world of the human spirit, of personhood and identity. It includes, but is by no means limited to, the rather common meaning of solitude in the dictionary: "The state of being alone." For Merton, interior solitude becomes in many places a metaphysical, ontological concept denoting man's ground of being, his inviolable incommunicable personality. In other places it is more of an inner atmosphere, a spiritual climate within man, a certain level of consciousness in which man confronts his inner depths. Interior solitude also refers to the journey within, the process of spiritual "emptying," the goal of which is the realization of one's transcendent identity, me as I am known by God, and as God intended me to be.

While physical solitude removes us from our fellow, interior solitude unites us with him. It is communion with our fellow on a much deeper level than the social fictions of life in a busy society or a technological world. Physical solitude is not absolutely necessary for the development of real interior solitude. As Merton said in one place:

> To love solitude and to seek it does not mean constantly traveling from one geographical possibility to another. A man becomes a solitary at the moment when, no matter what may be his external surroundings, he is

[1]Thomas Merton, *Seeds of Contemplation* (New York: New Directions, 1949), p. 42.

suddenly aware of his own inalienable solitude and sees that he will never be anything but solitary.[2]

I would like to ponder this one idea—that every person is a solitary. I would like to speak about the solitude of every person, the fear that many have of that reality and truth, and the need to be alone in order to discover our inner solitude.

MAN, THE SOLITARY

"Every man," Merton tells us, "is a solitary, held by the inexorable limitations of his own aloneness."[3] Each person experiences himself as an individual. I am like others, in that I share human nature with them. Yet I am not the other. I am distinct, separate, unique, alone. Nothing brings this home more forceably to us than the fact that we must die. For when each dies, he dies alone. Even if the dying person is surrounded in his last agony by the comforting presence of his loved ones, still, he is the one dying, and none of their words or affections can remove that reality from his consciousness. They in turn are reminded of what Merton calls "a mystery of living solitude," that is, that each one must also live alone. Death is the ultimate proof of one's aloneness.[4]

There is, too, an "awful solitude" in suffering, for "when a man suffers, he is most alone."[5] It is not simply the pain which reminds him of his solitariness. Certainly he alone must bear that pain. But, also, times of suffering often bring disturbing questions about the meaning of life. They

[2]Thomas Merton, *Thoughts In Solitude* (Garden City, New York: Image Books, 1968), p. 79.

[3]Thomas Merton, "Notes For a Philosophy of Solitude", *Disputed Questions*. (New York: Farrar, Straus and Cudahy, 1960), p. 181.

[4]Ibid., p. 181, and Thomas Merton, *Contemplation in a World of Action* (Garden City, New York: Doubleday and Company, 1971), p. 230.

[5]Thomas Merton, *No Man Is An Island*, (New York: Harcourt Brace, 1955), pp. 81, 85.

challenge a person to make sense of it all. Suddenly the apparently logical pattern of his well-organized and very rational life is shaken. There is a sense of contingency, insecurity, limitedness, helplessness, and a troubling anxiety about an unknown and unknowable future, all of which heighten the feeling of being alone.

Loneliness is probably the most common reminder that each person is solitary. It is a concrete experience of one's distinctness. Merton recognizes two basically different kinds of loneliness, though he uses no special terms to distinguish between them. The categories developed by Clark E. Moustakas capture Merton's variations in usage quite well.[6] Moustakas speaks of existential loneliness and anxiety loneliness. Existential loneliness is each person's experience of the reality of being human, of the human condition. In Merton's works it would include the loneliness of facing death and suffering mentioned before, of having to make crucial decisions about oneself or others for which one is responsible before God, of having to solve problems which are impossible to refer to the judgment of any other human being. It is the awareness found among married couples, who, for all their life and love shared, are still not completely one, and cannot be. Each stands alone, remains solitary. Existential loneliness is felt when one finally decides to stand on his own two feet and take responsibility for his own life. It is the acceptance of one's limitations and of the limitations of others. It involves what Merton calls "the lonely, barely comprehensible, incommunicable task" of facing the darkness of one's own mystery. In a word, existential loneliness is the realm of interior solitude and of the person. Notice how Merton uses the words *loneliness* and *solitude* interchangeably in this brief passage:

> If a man does not know the value of his own loneliness, how can he respect another's solitude?

[6]Clark E. Moustakas, *Loneliness*, (Englewood Cliffs, New Jersey: Prentice-Hall, 1961), pp. 33-34 and *Loneliness and Love*, (Englewood Cliffs, New Jersey; Prentice-Hall, 1972), p. 20.

> It is at once our loneliness and our dignity to have an
> incommunicable personality which is ours, ours alone
> and no one else's, and will be so forever.[7]

Anxiety loneliness, in contrast, is flight from existential
loneliness. It is the fear of loneliness: "The man who fears
to be alone will never be anything but lonely," Merton
says, "no matter how much he may surround himself with
people." Moustakas' description of anxiety loneliness
strikes so many chords which resonate in Merton's reflections on man as "individual" and man's "false self"
that is worth quoting:

> Anxiety loneliness would be the fear of loneliness, the
> desire to have a fundamental relationship with an other,
> but an inability to achieve or experience it; the result
> of a fundamental breach between what one is and what
> one pretends to be; a basic alienation between man and
> man and his nature, feelings of inferiority, easily hurt
> because so sensitive; efforts to escape it often result in
> giving up one's individuality, and a submergence in de-
> pendency relationships, and aggressiveness.[8]

Most people, Merton remarks, are "so averse to being
alone or feeling alone that they do everything they can to
forget their solitude.[9] They do anything they can to avoid
being alone and having to face themselves. They keep
busy, always on the go, organizing this or promoting that,
even under the guise of spreading the Kingdom of God.
They distract themselves with "divertissement," Pascal's
word for such diversions and systematic distractions, and
manage to avoid their own company for twenty-four hours
a day. If they are alone too long, or boredom raises its ugly
head, there is always something else to buy, another switch
to turn on, a bottle to open, a pill to swallow or a needle
to stick in.

[7]Merton, *No Man Is An Island*, p. 246.

[8]Moustakas, *Loneliness*, p. 24.

[9]Merton, "Notes For a Philosophy of Solitude", p. 178.

Why should a person be afraid to stop, to be silent, to be alone? When a person is quiet, and his quietness is not filled with day-dreams or plans for more distractions, he comes face to face with himself in the lonely ground of his own being. He becomes increasingly aware of the presence within himself of a disturbing stranger, the self that is both "I" and "someone else," a self that is not entirely welcome because it is so unlike the more familiar everyday self of distracted living.

Questions emerge about the value of one's existence, the reality of one's commitments, the authenticity of one's everyday life. A person begins to experience what he has been trying so hard to avoid, a sense of anguish and dread, the sense of nothingness that assails him as soon as he is left alone. Often there is a feeling of isolation and of being unlovable. He doesn't know if there is anything in himself worthy even of respect, since he has never paused long enough to find out. Thus a wave of emptiness and self-hate may sweep over him. This is a crucial moment for man, the solitary. Merton calls it the first "difficulty" of interior solitude; that is:

> The disconcerting task of facing and accepting one's own absurdity. The anguish of realizing that underneath the apparently logical pattern of a more or less "well organized" and rational life, there lies an abyss of irrationality, confusion, pointlessness, and indeed of apparent chaos.[10]

Obviously it is an anxious and anguishing moment. It is all the more so, since this kind of anguish has no definite object. Rather, it is a confrontation with the void, with emptiness, nothingness, a feeling of spiritual disorientation.

For many, these anxieties which arise out of the existential loneliness of man are just too much to face. To accept oneself as solitary is too frightening. In his eagerness to set his subjective anxieties at rest, a person is in danger of selling himself out to anything that will give him a

[10]Ibid., p. 179.

semblance of peace, no matter how deceptive. His rebellion against this loneliness (true interior solitude) drives him proudly to assert himself, to affirm himself by power over people or things in the hope that power and possessions will sustain his illusory self-image by giving him some identity. Instead, such ploys only deepen an abiding sense of isolation. Such a person continues to live according to an illusion, and, says Merton, "ultimately he who lives for and by such an illusion must end either in disgust or madness."[11] In fleeing from loneliness, he flees from himself and from God. Merton relates this to the doctrine of original sin, which he describes as "a spontaneous inclination to resolve the split in ourselves by denying that it exists, and by closing ourselves in upon the superficial and exterior unity of the superficial ego."[12] This flight and denial are the core of anxiety loneliness.

The existential experience of one's solitariness, with all its anguish and anxiety, is a call for a person to discover the meaning of his life. This, above all, is a solitary task, for while others can assist, support, and guide, each person must take the responsibility for living his or her own life and for finding him/herself." Merton says:

> If he persists in shifting this responsibility to someone else, he fails to find the meaning of his own existence. You cannot tell me who I am, and I cannot tell you who you are. If you do not know your own identity, who is going to identify you? Others can give you a name or a number, but they can never tell you who you really are. That is something only you yourself can discover from within.[13]

Yet we do live in society. We grow up and learn about life by living with and like others. We begin at our birth to assimilate our own *meaning* by observing other peoples'

[11]Thomas Merton, "A Conference on Prayer, *Sisters Today* 41 (April, 1970), p. 26.

[12]Thomas Merton, *Opening The Bible*, (Collegeville, Minnesota: Liturgical Press, 1971), p. 72.

[13]Merton, *No Man Is An Island*, p. xii.

meanings being acted out in their lives. Unfortunately there is a natural laziness in us which, without our even knowing it, urges us to avoid the difficult task of working through our own identities. We tend to flee from our own solitude, from the implications of being unique, distinct, having an incommunicable personality which is ours, ours alone, and no one else's. We avoid it by accepting others' answers to the problem of life and our own identity. This is a lot easier, less threatening and precarious, than entering into the darkness of our own solitude to search there for our own special *meaning*. The result is often the surrender of what is deepest and most essential to oneself, and a consequent conformity to a social image, a kind of collective identity.

Merton had a lot to say about this way of solving our identity question. He felt that one of the most characteristic ways we evade the identity problem is "conformism, running with the herd, the refusal of solitude and the flight from loneliness."[14] We have a society that for all its unquestionable advantages and fantastic ingenuity, just does not seem to be able to provide people with lives that are fully human and fully real.

We do not grow up in a vacuum, nor do we establish our identities entirely on our own. Our way of looking at life, and interpreting ourselves, is not something we create all by ourselves out of nothing. Our ways of thinking, our values, and even our attitudes toward ourselves, are influenced by the surrounding society and culture. Since any society wants to bring a person to the point where he or she can participate in the aspirations, needs, and desires of that group, it naturally presents its own ideal of what it means to be a person, what it means to be happy and fulfilled. It is really possible, and Merton felt it was becoming more and more actual today, that we could arrive at adulthood having so absorbed society's slogans and concepts that they become so much a part of us that they rise spontaneously from us as if they were our own ideas. So a

[14]Merton, *Contemplation In a World of Action*, p. 42.

person becomes a member of what Merton called "Mass Mind," "Mass Society," a member of the collectivity.

One of the things Merton observed in our culture is its narcissism. It is interested only in the affirmation of self, and in the fulfillment of the self's own limited needs and desires. It encourages us to create an awareness of ourselves as people who have no needs we cannot immediately satisfy. The really real becomes the superficial, the sensual, the "I" isolated in self. Obviously, to exist on this level you have to suppress the awareness of your unreality and radical need. You are urged to enjoy yourself, to try any of the million diversions in society that will quiet existential anxiety.

Existential anxiety, however, is not so easily put aside. So society steps in even more quickly with a larger and more diversified bag of tricks to relieve the more persistent soundings of the inner self. A person can easily get caught up in the ever-repeating cycle of anxiety, diversions, more anxiety and unrest . . . . Thus we have alienation.

The only way out is to face and accept one's own solitariness and loneliness. This, of course, brings pain. But it also brings possibilities. Anxiety remains and probably will never disappear completely. But it is not the self-sorrowing, fearful, even neurotic anxiety of anxiety loneliness. It is rather the pain of existential loneliness, a healthy pain, Merton says, caused by the blocking of vital energies that still remain for radical change. In other words, though pain is definitely present, it holds the promise of something new. The pain of existential loneliness and existential anxiety call us beyond our familiar societal self to take responsibility for our own inner lives, and so to become real persons. It is the pain that comes in our freely accepting our own absurdity and insecurity. It is the pain of dread—that pervading awareness that somehow we have not lived up to our own inner truth. But the possibilities are enormous: meaning coming out of our meaninglessness, peace and understanding and self-acceptance out of our anguish.

In this process, solitude serves as the medium, the

atmosphere, the catalyst, the doorway, the path, to true inner solitude. I have to learn to be alone, to accept the solitude which is myself, in order to be myself. I have to learn to quiet myself so that I can hear the voice of that deeper, truer me which cries for understanding and love. I have to learn to be alone if I am going to face the illusions and delusions I have fashioned for myself or have unknowingly or unquestioningly accepted from my surroundings. I have to learn to trust myself to solitude, so that I can discover true solitude.

Merton, in the following poem, assures us that solitude itself will be our guide to our inner truth, and that out of the pain and the darkness of solitude come the joys of solitude:

> If you seek a heavenly light,
>   I, Solitude, am your professor.
>
> I go before you into emptiness,
>   Raise strange suns for your new mornings,
> Opening the secret windows of your innermost apartment.
>
> When I, Loneliness, give my special signal,
>   Follow my silence, follow where I beckon.
> Fear not, little beast, little spirit,
>   (thou word and animal)
> I, Solitude, am Angel
>   And have prayed in your name.
>
> Look at the empty, wealthy night,
>   The pilgrim moon!
> I am the appointed hour,
>   The "now" that cuts time like a blade.
>
> I am the unexpected flash beyond "yes", beyond "no".
>   The forerunner of the word of God.
>
> Follow my ways and I will lead you to golden-haired
>   suns, Logos, and music, blameless joys, innocent of
>   question and beyond answers.
>
> For I, Solitude, am thine own Self:

I, Nothingness, am thy all.
I, Silence, am thy Amen.[15]

II. Solitude: Our Guide to Inner Reality

"If you seek a heavenly light, I, Solitude, am your Professor." With these words Thomas Merton sums up his vision of the role solitude plays in our lives. If we truly seek the Lord, and the deeper realities of life, we must become disciples of Solitude. We must learn to be alone, to sit at Solitude's feet, and allow this Professor, our spiritual guide, to lead us into the solitude of God.

The beauty of Merton's reflections on the meaning and value of solitude comes, I believe, from the realization that these are no heady reflections, no mere theories, but flow from the lived reality of his own life. Certainly Merton was steeped in the Monastic and Desert Fathers. He had the knack of capturing the wisdom of ancient writings and making it apply to us today. But there was little of this ancient wisdom on solitude that he had not experienced himself. When he commented on the flight from solitude in our contemporary society, he did it with the realization that he had once been a part of that flight. But now he could write with the insight his Professor, Solitude, had given him.

It was soon after his conversion, when he first began to think of becoming a priest, that the idea of solitude started to exert a kind of magnetic attraction upon his whole being. He felt drawn to solitude as his place in the world, that sacred space where he could best become himself, and best become all that God wanted him to be. He gradually came to realize that going off to the solitude of a Trappist monastery, secluded in the hills of Kentucky, was hardly a flight from anyone or anything. On the contrary, it was a headlong dash straight forward, to seek someone, to seek God alone in the desert.

[15]Thomas Merton, untitled poem, *The Solitary Life*, (Lexington, Kentucky: Stamperis del Santuccio, 1969, private printing), frontpiece.

A man who had lived with Merton and had been trained as a monk under him once remarked: "To his close acquaintances, Father Merton's name and the term *solitude* are correlatives,"[16] so much did Merton speak about solitude. But in Merton's own experience, I think it would be more accurate to say that *solitude* and *God* were correlatives: to seek God was to seek solitude; to seek solitude was to seek God. Solitude was such a driving force in his own life, and became such an integral part of all that he wrote, because it was in solitude that he sought and found God. In 1950, he wrote to a friend: "My heart consents to nothing but God and solitude."[17] Some fifteen years later, and about a week after he finally realized his desire to take up full time residence in the ultimate solitude of a hermitage, the theme was the same. He wrote: "I have rapidly discovered that what I am seeking here in the hermitage is not eremitism or spirituality or contemplation, but simply God."[18] It is the voice of experience and conviction that says to us: "If you seek a heavenly light, I, Solitude, am your Professor."

We remember how it was when Merton first began writing about solitude. He burst upon us in 1948 with *The Seven Storey Mountain*, and we were amazed that such a cosmopolitan, multi-talented young man could give up a promising future to shut himself up in a contemplative monastery. But it was also obvious that he had found there a peace, a sense of fulfillment in commitment to ultimates that we all long for.

When he followed up with another personal journal, *The Sign of Jonas*, he shared with us the longing of his heart, and our hearts, for a closer union with the Lord. He explained the ideals of solitude and the monastic life in *The Waters of Siloe* and *The Silent Life*. He did it in such an appealing way that many young people began to see that

---

[16]Gerald Groves, "My Fourteen Years with Thomas Merton", *The Critic* 21 (April-May 1963), p. 30.

[17]From a letter to Sister Lentfoehr in Patrick Hart (edition), *Thomas Merton/ Monk* (New York: Sheed and Ward, 1974), p. 106.

[18]Letter of 30 August 1965 to Dom Winandy (Thomas Merton Study Center Collection).

kind of life as a real option for them. To an even wider public he opened the world of interior solitude with *Seeds of Contemplation* and *No Man Is An Island*. During those first ten years of publishing, he became one of the most popular spiritual writers of the day. He revealed to an activity-oriented American Church and to busy people in a harried and hurrying society the inner world of the spirit, where God dwells in solitude, waiting for us to slow down enough to enter his solitude.

The 1960's, however, brought a whole new set of challenges. Now the task was not so much to explain the values of solitude as to defend its very right to exist in the Church and in the world. The growing call for more involvement in the world reached the whole Church in Vatican II's discussion and directives. Already a cautious, even curious, topic for many, solitude began to appear regressive, a flight from the world, a too personalistic approach to God, a betrayal of responsibilities, a kind of ostrich "head-in-the-sand" approach toward God at work in the world. Interrestingly, it was about 1960 that the Trappists themselves, committed as they were to a communal life in solitude, allowed Merton to write freely about the hermit's life. So, beginning in 1960, Merton renewed his efforts to reveal the importance of solitude for an authentic human life, as well as to emphasize to the monks themselves that solitude was an essential characteristic of their vocation. It was not only the monastic, contemplative life that was at stake, but the appreciation of solitude itself. Just a year before he died, as late as 1967, Merton said: "The defense of the contemplative life today implies also the defense of solitude."[19]

Merton turned to Scripture to show the importance solitude played in Salvation History. It was in the solitude of the desert, at Horeb, that Moses saw the burning bush and heard the call which began the ultimate salvific event of the Old Testament. It was to the desert that the Lord

[19]Thomas Merton, "The Solitary Life", *Cistercian Studies* 4 (1969): no. 3, p. 213.

brought his people, to covenant with them. After their sin at Sinai, the Lord kept his people in the desert, in order, as Hosea puts it, "to allure her and speak to her tenderly." In the desert the people learned how to live in faith and with dependence on Yahweh, to follow his lead, and most especially, to learn how to love him. Mary, alone at prayer, heard the angel's message, and her "fiat" changed all history. It was John the Baptist, baptizing at the Jordan on the edge of the desert, who was the first to recognize the Messiah. It was to the desert that the Lord went, led by the Spirit, there to struggle against the Evil one with his deceptive promises of security, reputation, and power.

We find Jesus withdrawing alone, or with a few choice friends, even in the midst of his apostolic work. It was immediately after such a solitary stay on the Mount of Transfiguration that Jesus resolutely set his face toward Jerusalem, with all the consequences that would bring. And it was in the quiet and solitude of the Garden of Olives that Jesus recommitted himself to the Father's will and the morrow's events. All these solitary moments were crucial in the history of God's actions toward us, and crucial for understanding God's ways with us.

Merton was well aware of these biblical foundations for solitude, and pointed them out particularly to the monks, who were direct descendants of those Christians who through the ages went out into the desert to seek God alone. But Merton was also in touch with the pulse of his own day. He found he shared much with those existentialists who were acutely aware of the subtle process by which a person today loses himself in the vast emptiness of a public or common mentality. Instead of a society made up of unique, free individuals, there is Mass Man, Mass Society today. Merton called on each person to move toward authentic existence which can only begin when a person decides to exist truly and freely, that is, when he accepts his own finiteness and his own limitations, his own aloneness, as well as his own dignity, as a matter of personal choice.

Let me illustrate this with Merton's own words. Merton

outlined the plot of a play from the Theater of the Absurd, Ionesco's *Rhinoceros*, in this way: Berenger, the leading character, discovers one day that all of his fellow citizens, all his friends, and even his girl friend Daisy, have turned into rhinoceroses. "When Berenger suddenly finds himself the last human in a rhinoceros herd," Merton says, "he looks into a mirror and says, humbly enough, 'After all, man is not as bad as all that, is he?' But his world now shakes mightily under the stampede of his metamorphosed fellow citizens . . . he looks in the mirror and sees that he no longer resembles anyone. He searches madly for a photograph of people as they were before the big change. But now humanity itself has become incredible, as well as hideous. To be the last man in the rhinoceros herd is, in fact, to be a monster."[20]

Merton then comments: "Such is the problem Ionesco sets before us in his tragic irony: solitude and dissent become more and more impossible, more and more tragic." He then lets Ionesco speak for himself. "In all the cities of the world," says the playwright, "it is the same. The universal and modern man is the man in a rush (that is, a rhinoceros), a man who has no time, who is a prisoner of necessity, who cannot understand that a thing might perhaps be without usefulness; nor does he understand that, at bottom, it is the useful that may be a useless and back-breaking burden . . . ." (and isn't solitude useless, non-productive, a waste of time?). "Rhinoceritis," he adds, "is the sickness that lies in wait for those who have lost the sense and the taste for solitude."[21]

That is exactly Merton's position: Without a certain degree of solitude, we lose our sense of wonder and get caught in a world where only the practical and the useful count; we do not know to think for ourselves, but can only run with the stampeding herd. We change. And the "odd man out" turns out to be the only true person. The rest of

[20]Thomas Merton, "Rain and the Rhinoceros", *Raids on the Unspeakable*, (New York: New Directions, 1966), pp. 19-21.

[21]Ibid., p. 21.

us have become rhinoceroses. We are just too afraid to be alone, too afraid to work through the mystery of who we really are. So we surrender ourselves to society, to some cause, to some other person, hoping that this "other" can give us an identity and tell us who we are.

We need a certain degree of solitude, of stepping back from the crowd, to get in touch with ourselves, to think for ourselves, to get below the superficial, to see the subtle influences our friends, our society, have on us. How are we ever going to be our own person if we never pause long enough to listen to ourselves? How can we avoid being a rhinoceros, one with Mass Mind, unless we separate ourselves to some extent, to get a clearer perspective of things and of what is happening around us? We have to develop some sense of solitude, some taste for solitude, if we want to discover who we are, and what God is saying to us. This is what Merton means by interior solitude: Being a whole person, having a relatively firm grasp on one's own identity, an inner togetherness, a sense of one's dignity as God's child.

In an anxious age like ours, Merton was convinced that many people will have to face the need for interior solitude and silence, "simply to keep themselves together, to maintain their human Christian identity and their spiritual freedom."[22] He suggests that everyone seek out moments of silence, of meditation, and of quiet peace. These help promote an inner atmosphere of "being in touch," of reflective pondering, of quiet peace within, even in the midst of crowds.

Therefore, physical solitude and silence contribute to the humanizing and personalizing of man, and so are necessary, to some extent, Merton says, for the fullness of human living: "Not all men are called to be hermits, but all men need enough silence and solitude in their lives to enable the deep inner voice of their own true self to be heard at least occasionally. When that inner voice is not heard, when man cannot attain to the spiritual peace that comes from

[22]Thomas Merton, *Contemplative Prayer* (New York: Herder and Herder, 1969), p. 20.

being perfectly at one with his true self, his life is always miserable and exhausting. For he cannot go on happily for long unless he is in contact with the springs of spiritual life which are hidden in the depths of his own soul."[23]

In the late 1960's, Merton observed that more and more people were turning to silence and solitude, not in order to plan, organize, or think in an analytic way, but simply in order to BE.

SILENCE

They want to get themselves together in silence. They want to synthesize, to integrate themselves, to rediscover themselves in a unity of thought, will, understanding, and love. Silence is the proper atmosphere for inner seeking. It shuts out the noise and tensions of a busy world as it relaxes the mind and body. Silence is healing: "Not only does silence give us a chance to understand ourselves better, to get a truer and more balanced perspective of our own lives in relation to the lives of others; silence makes us whole if we let it. Silence helps draw together the scattered and dissipated energies of a fragmented existence. It helps us to concentrate on a purpose that really corresponds not only to the deepest needs of our own being, but also to God's intentions for us."[24]

Morton Kelsey, in his beautiful book, *The Other Side of Silence*, tells a vivid story of Karl Jung that illustrates the healing power of silence. A clergyman came to see Dr. Jung. His nerves were frazzled. He was on the ragged side of breaking down. He had been working fourteen hours a day. Jung told him the only thing he wanted him to do was this: sleep eight hours a day, work only eight hours, then spend the remaining hours all alone in your den, in quiet. The next day the clergyman tried it. He slept his eight hours, and quit work after he had put in eight hours,

---

[23]Thomas Merton, *The Silent Life* (New York: Farrar, Straus and Cudahy, 1957), p. 167.

[24]Thomas Merton, "Creative Silence", *The Baptist Student* 48 (February 1969), p. 21.

then retired to his den and shut the door. He played a few Chopin Etudes, and finished a Herman Hesse novel. The next day he did the same thing, except this time he read Thomas Mann's *Magic Mountain* and played a Mozart Sonata. The third day he went back to see Dr. Jung, complaining that he was just as bad off as before; and he obviously was!

When Jung heard how he had spent his evenings, he said, "But you didn't understand! I didn't want you to be with Herman Hesse or Thomas Mann, or even Mozart or Chopin. I wanted you to be all alone with yourself." At this the minister looked terrified, and gasped, "Oh, but I can't think of any worse company!" To which Dr. Jung replied, "But isn't this the self you inflict on other people fourteen hours a day?"[25]

More important for the Christian, silence and solitude, which nurture solitude of heart, are the proper climate for waiting for God, for listening attentively for his word to be spoken in us. Merton says that "we listen to the Father best in solitude."[26] A certain amount of silence and solitude is good, becaue it is in silence, and not in commotion, Merton says, in solitude and not in crowds, that God best likes to reveal himself most intimately to us. Silence and solitude help us to see ourselves as we are in God's eyes, to see our need for God's mercy and grace, and to recover some of the spiritual powers which are ours in the Holy Spirit because of our union with Christ.

There is a wonderful interplay of external solitude and silence, and inner silence and solitude of heart. Physical solitude and silence are necessary, to some extent, for the voice of the inner self to be heard. They provide a hospitable and nourishing atmosphere in which the work of inner journeying can take place. They help us to experience our aloneness, our uniqueness, and to face ourselves.

As we grow more comfortable in our inner world and get in touch with who we are and who God is for us, we often

[25]Morton Kelsey, *The Other Side of Silence*
[26]Merton, *Thoughts In Solitude*, p. 102.

seem drawn toward more exterior solitude and silence. Speaking of that deep interior prayer in which the Spirit eventually seems to take over one's prayer life, Merton says: "Such prayer draws us naturally to interior and even exterior solitude. It does not depend on exterior conditions, but it has effected such an interior isolation and solitariness in our own souls that we naturally tend to seek silence and solitude for our bodies and for our souls. And it is good for the soul to be in solitude for a great part of the time."[27]

Periods of exterior solitude and silence help us sustain our own personal authenticity and truth at the same time as they assist us to renew our commitment of love to God and our brothers and sisters.

Interior solitude and silence, in turn, assure that the separation from others which is involved in exterior solitude is itself authentic. For it is quite possible that someone will separate himself from others simply because one dislikes them, or has rejected them, or wants to escape from them. Maybe one has been frustrated in love, discouraged by life, is afraid of involvement with people or issues. Perhaps one is simply seeking some extraordinary contemplative powers, or simply seeking notice. Merton works hard to express and reject these false motivations, which render solitude sterile and positively dangerous.

Merton insists over and over again that the best criterion for judging whether separation from others is valid and interior solitude authentic, is this: that true solitude helps us to forget ourselves, breaks through our concentration on self, and helps us reach out in practical love to our brothers and sisters. Far from being a flight from the world, true solitude sends us into the world with a new vision, new motivation, new dynamism, to be Christ's leaven in the world and to incarnate his love in our time, in our place.

Just going off alone will not accomplish all of this. It is a good start. Physical solitude may assist interior solitude, but it is not identified with it. Rather, physical solitude

[27]Merton, *No Man Is An Island*, p. 50.

and silence join a host of other elements, such as prayer, self-denial, and positive acts of charity, of reaching out, in developing true interior solitude. Nonetheless, in Merton's mind, exterior solitude was crucial for anyone who sought God, and he protested against any down-playing of or dismissal of physical solitude as unnecessary. "How can people act and speak as if solitude were a matter of little importance in the interior life? Only those who have never experienced real solitude can glibly declare that it 'makes no difference,' and that only solitude of the heart really matters! One solitude must lead to the other!"[28]

See how in the following short passage Merton begins with solitude as a physical reality, and then moves quickly into interior solitude in its fullness: "Is it true to say that one goes into solitude to 'get at the root of existence'? It would be better to say that in solitude one *is* at the root. He who is alone and is conscious of what his solitude means, finds himself simply in the ground of life. He is 'in love'."[29] He is in God, who is Love.

"If you seek a heavenly light, I, Solitude, am your Professor." Thomas Merton studied long and fruitfully at the feet of his master, Solitude. It was his experience of solitude which led him down to his very center, where he discovered not only his deepest identity, but God Himself, and, in God, all people. Modern spiritual writers such as Catherine de Hueck Doherty, Henri Nouwen, Edward Farrell or Carlo Carretto—all have gone to solitude to learn. Ask any one who has gone off for a desert experience alone, or has made a directed retreat. They will tell you the same thing as Merton: If you seek a heavenly light, you will not find a better Professor than Solitude.

I end by quoting from Merton's last circular letter to his friends: "I shall continue to feel bound to all of you in the silence of prayer. Our real journey in life is interior: it is a

---

[28]Thomas Merton, *New Seeds of Contemplation*, (New York: New Directions, 1962), p. 80.

[29]Thomas Merton, "Love and Solitude", *The Critic* 25 (October-November 1966), p. 36.

matter of growth, of deepening and of an ever greater surrender to the creative action of love and grace in our hearts. Never was it more necessary for us to respond to that action. I pray that we all may do so. God bless you. With all affection in Christ. Thomas Merton."[30]

[30]Thomas Merton, *The Asian Journal of Thomas Merton*, (New York: New Directions, 1973), p. 296.

4

PIECES OF THE MOSAIC, EARTH: THOMAS MERTON AND THE CHRIST

George Kilcourse

The Cistercian monk-poet had seemingly anticipated this focus of his Christocentric spirituality when he recapitulated his contribution to the dedication of the Thomas Merton Studies Center at Bellarmine College.:

> Whatever I have written, I think all can be reduced in the end to this one root truth: that God calls human persons to union with himself and with one another in Christ . . . .

A shelf of books and several hundred magazine articles, reviews, and thousands of letters later, the chronicle of that Merton literature traces the pilgrimage of Merton's encounter with and reflections on Christ. My purpose is to offer some systematic reading of that image and understanding of Merton's Christocentric spirituality. Certain peaks and definite Christological veins define Merton's reflections on Christ. The bulk of my observations will attempt to identify and to systematize that Christological vision.

In one sense, what I will attempt in this exploration-survey will not afford any "new" insights. The Benedictine, Jean LeClercq, encourages us in this conviction as he nominates Merton for mention "with the Fathers of the Early Church and those of the Middle Ages." "Not only, as do all Christians, did he live the same mystery as they did, but he lived and expressed it in the same way." His humanism, LeClercq ventures, just as that of the Fathers, "drew from the culture of their own times in order to make it a part of their inner experience."

Rather, what endures in this legacy of Merton's monastic instincts and spirituality is the *experience* of Christ as the center of his extraordinary reflections for a contemporary and transitional epoch.

We might venture to style this chapter as a "revisionist" scrutiny of Merton's Christological thought. And, indeed, we find familiar and orthodox formulas, the anticipated signposts and vernacular through which he engaged with contemporary theological ferment. But having termed the character of this investigation "revisionist," one wonders: Is it already incumbent upon us to re-focus the Merton portrait? I think so. For the hagiographers and image-artificers already have set about sculpting a towering figure of the twentieth century's most famous monk. And, much to Merton's chagrin—though he appeared more and more resigned to the inevitability—that is expected, even necessary, for a figure of reliable yet creative transition in a world of turmoil. It is, however, when we examine the features of that likeness to Merton that inquiry begins.

Is the Thomas Merton, whom much of the literature and critical surveys present, recognizable? What about the contours and gestures, the postures attributed to Merton by his image-makers?

There remains a staggering interdisciplinary task ahead in systematizing and integrating the multi-faceted personality of Thomas Merton. I like to image the integral Mertonian vision as something like the six vantage-points or faces of a cube: Monk, Mystic, Poet, Social Critic, Theologian, and Humanist. From each of these at times scattered Mertonian enthusiasms, the mystery of Christ radiates.

The project of systematizing and correlating Merton's work remains complicated by his eclectic habit. He was, by nature, spontaneous, addressing questions and discussions as an *essayist*. Readers need only examine the genesis of his books—collections of essays, articles quilted together "topically" and (at times) loosely fashioned into a single volume. Likewise, the *journal* style remained a tool implanted from his early French and British habitat. While the immediacy of a personal, autobiographical dimension remains the power of Merton's writing, much "occasional" Merton grates uncomfortably against the larger, especially later spirituality. Theology as "story," we hear more loudly today, is the reliable method. Witness the entrance of Merton to notoriety in the modern version of Augustine's "Confessions," his *The Seven Storey Mountain*. And yet, even the hazards and limits of this essayist-journalist-autobiographer tradition caught up with Merton.

"Perspective" and "context" remain keys in our approach to Merton. Let us label it formally—the hermeneutical task we bring to Merton's work. He voiced this very concern in a 1967 interview. He was willing to "accept *The Seven Storey Mountain* as a point of departure," but more anxious to "depart from it and keep moving."

> I left the book behind many years ago. Certainly it was a book I had to write, and it says a great deal of what I have to say: but if I had to write it over again, it would be handled in a very different way, and in a different idiom. It is a youthful book, too simple, in many ways, too crude. Everything is laid out in black and white . . . I still did not understand the real problems of the monastic life, or even of the Christian life. And I was still dealing in a crude theology that I had learned as a novice: a clean-cut division between the natural and supernatural, God and the world, sacred and secular, with boundary lines that were supposed to be quite evident . . . . Unfortunately, the book was a best-seller, and has become a kind of edifying legend . . . I am doing my best to live it down . . . . I rebel against it and maintain my basic human right *not* to be turned into a Catholic myth for children in parochial schools.

It is similarly the "Humanity of God" in Christ that Merton tenaciously refused to turn into a "myth" (I use the word cautiously, with Merton's meaning here, an unreliable rendition) for Christians. It is at the intersection of autobiography and theology that Merton's consistent presentation of the Christ mystery finds its extraordinary devotional impact.

It was the Columbia University philosophy professor, Daniel Clark Walsh, Merton's spiritual father, who captured this essential Merton in the homily he gave at Gethsemani ten years ago (December 17, 1968) for Merton's funeral. He spoke of "what I personally regard as his true greatness: that deep and abiding sense of God in Christ, and of God in man through Christ; of Christ in his Church; Christ in each of us through the action of his Holy Spirit; the Christ of God who in the Spirit of his love lives in the people of God; the Christ who is in us when we love and serve one another in true brotherhood—when we realize that we are not our brother's keeper but our brother's brother."

Without detailing the pilgrimage of Merton's Christological thought (and perhaps it does not warrant the formal, systematic nomenclature of a "Christology"), I discover a continuity, richly developed, in Merton's writing about the Christ. Let us turn to the peaks and lifelines of that journey.

The Seven Storey Mountain rehearses for us his discovery of the Christ. It is his guru, Dan Walsh, who stirs the waters of Merton's new life in Christ. By dubbing Merton an "Augustinian," Walsh located Merton's larval theological mind. Thomas Merton grew enthused with the prospect of being in the spiritual company of Bonaventure, Scotus, and Anselm—a "spiritual, mystical, voluntaristic, and practical way" of spirituality, distinct from Aquinas' speculative school. As an Augustinian, Merton discovered that his relationship to God was in the order of pure love. As Dan Walsh expressed this tradition: it was a philosophy of the *Person*. The lineage of Merton's spirituality emerges. Under the mentorship of Etienne

Gilson, Walsh had written his doctoral dissertation on Duns Scotus and his philosophy. This Franciscan strain of medieval philosophy and theology became the crossroads of Merton's later reflections on the Christ. On the question of "Why the 'redemption'? What is the primary reason for the Son of God becoming man?" Scotus' point of departure is radically distinct from that of Saint Thomas. For Scotus, Incarnation is inevitable because of Love; for Thomas, Incarnation is *necessary* to redeem us.

This Scotist contribution to Christology echoes the Church's patristic thinkers—the Greek Fathers—with their intuition of the cosmic Christ. A confidence in creation, grace building on nature, stood waiting for Merton's discovery—what I call Merton's later "raids on the tradition," his Patristic research in the nineteen fifties issuing in books like *The New Man* (1961) and *New Seeds of Contemplation* (1961).

In fact, there is an account of one of Merton's prior experiences that images this link with the Christology of the Greek Fathers. In nascent form he pondered, he says, "for the first time in my life . . . who this Person was that man called Christ." It was during his eighteenth year, 1933, while vacationing in Rome before beginning his riotous year at Cambridge. Bored with the ruins of pagan Rome, he gravitated uncomprehendingly to the cathedrals and the churches. There he confronted the *mosaics*, those unique Roman forms of art that expressed in their own way the iconic Eastern Empire traditions of imaging the Christ.

> These mosaics told me more than I had ever known of the doctrines of a God of infinite power, wisdom and love, who had yet become Man, and revealed in his Manhood the infinity of power, wisdom and love that was his Godhead . . . I grasped them implicitly—I had to, in so far as the mind of the artist reached my own mind and spoke to it his conception of his thought.

A sermon at Corpus Christi Church, while he was a Columbia student flirting with Catholicism, dramatized this same mystery of Incarnation. The experience of this central Christian mystery transformed Merton. He "looked about . . . at a new world," where all was transfigured, even the ugly facades of Broadway and Columbia's environs.

At the same time, without exercising that ecumenical sensitivity he later developed, Merton rejected Huxley's philosophy because "in discarding his family's tradition of materialism, he had followed the old Protestant groove back into the heresies that make the material creation evil of itself." Merton could not tolerate such seeming suspicion of the doctrine of Incarnation.

It is, at first, a curious turn for an Augustinian. We might expect more Platonism—but as Jean LeClercq points out, Merton had the ability to go to the essence of a passage (or author) and make it his own. The primacy of Love is his legacy of Augustine. As Abbot Flavian Burns of Gethsemani pointed out in his homily at the death of Dan Walsh (he died on the feast of Saint Augustine, August 28, 1976), one of the Augustinian texts Dan most frequently shared with his students was: "God is more intimate to me than I am to myself." Incarnation communicated the totality of that intimacy in Merton's understanding of God's love.

In his 1938 thesis on William Blake, Merton discovered the incarnational dynamic that achieves Beauty. The mystic-poet looks through matter into eternity. "Clarity" is the "glory of form shining through matter." And the route became even more directly Incarnational and Christological in his sortie into the poetry of Gerard Manley Hopkins, the intended subject of his doctoral dissertation. The Scotist link, a Franciscan-Bonaventurean heritage, is germane to any serious study of Hopkins (although we have precious little outside of Merton's own poetry to trace his appreciation of Hopkins and to judge the degree to which he was influenced by the Jesuit).

Where does the pilgrimage of Merton go from Columbia University? There was the brief teaching stint at Saint Bonaventure's, and the struggle with a career in Catholic Worker activity. Finally, three days after the ordeal of

Pearl Harbor, Merton was walking through the arch of Gethsemani Abbey. Almost a decade passed before we got much of a glimpse of his life cloistered in monastic silence. And what irony greeted his autobiography! Fame and celebrity shadowed him from that literary event!

The questions we pose are gathered into a focal inquiry: What had monastic experience and formation contributed to Merton's spirituality? Certainly the liturgical and communal life heightened his insight into Christ. And the contemplative and mystical traditions were a quiet oasis from which Merton drank deeply. Through the forties and well into the decade of the fifties, Merton raided the Christian tradition—by osmosis and absorption. When that burlap-covered volume, *Seeds of Contemplation*, appeared, the contours of a personally-adapted spirituality, an idiom, were defined. The contemplative questions were curled into the search: "Who am I?" Major directions in his spirituality were announced in the ascetic journey; solitude, integrity, humility, liberty, detachment, and renunciation were traced in chapters addressed to an audience "in the world." Monks, he claims, quest to discover their own true selves in Christ. This, he continues, is the only reason for entering the monastery—to experience the *mercy* of God. The dynamics of this "transforming union" that the monk experiences are the life project of denying an illusory, false self. The action of God's love for us (the Incarnate Christ) calls us to be a unique person and, in that discovery of "who" we are *in Christ*, to give glory to him.

> You seem to be the same person and you are the same person that you have always been; in fact, you are more yourself than you have ever been before. You have only just begun to exist. You feel as if you were at last fully born. All that went before was a mistake, a fumbling preparation for birth. Now you have come into your own element. And yet now you have become nothing. You have sunk to the center of your own poverty... You are free to go in and out of infinity.

The motif of this declaration—new life!—is one familiar in Merton, playing on the Christ-event as an "emptying," the *kenosis* of the ancient Pauline hymn in Philippians (2:5-11). In an important chapter of *Seeds of Contemplation*, entitled "Through a Glass," Merton images the cosmic existence of God's humanity in Christ. He reflects on this mystical intuition of the "magnifying glass" of Christ's Humanity concentrating the "rays of God's light and fire to a point that sets fire to the spirit of man."

A wealth of Christological material weaves through this text. In the next major work, *The Ascent to Truth*, a harmonious chord is struck. This is a curious work in one way, in its method, employing scholastic theology and vocabulary. Merton attempts to juxtapose John of the Cross' mysticism and the system of Thomas Aquinas. While ponderous and at times pedantic in style, the work is significant as a defense of mysticism (Gregory of Nyssa and John of the Cross) against popular caricatures of Gnosticism or anti-incarnational spirituality. Incarnation—God's humanity—recurs like a refrain in this study. "God's revelation of himself to the world in his Incarnate Word forms the heart and substance of all Christian mystical contemplation," he concludes. A radical transformation of consciousness is the response to Christ. The dramatic imagery of Merton's prose-poetry puts it thus: "God must move and reveal himself and shake the world within the soul and rise from his sleep like a giant." The mystic is transformed "like a bar of iron in the heat of a furnace." Humanity is not destroyed, but transfigured.

The books that issued from the cell at Gethsemani in the fifties, *The Last of the Fathers* (1954), *No Man Is An Island* (1955), *Thoughts in Solitude* (1958), return to an idiom of personal reflection, a dialogue with the reader that signaled Merton's refusal ever to return to the theological "voice" of scholasticism. He calls the reflections "personal" and avows "leaving systems to others." (Though he continued to research and study the contemporary theological literature, he was uncomfortable with its academic distancing.)

Marian reflections in his study of Bernard of Clairvaux (*The Last of the Fathers*) are the threshold for reflections on Christ. But a key is recovered in the other two works. "Person" is the recovery of my "deepest self," recovery of identity in Christ. "The meaning of my life," he insists, "is seen, above all, in my integration in the mystery of Christ." Again, the affirmation of the goodness of creation, the material world, is announced.

The incarnational motif continues in *Thoughts in Solitude*. If we are to become spiritual, we must remain men. And if there were not evidence of this everywhere in theology, the Mystery of the Incarnation itself would be ample proof of it." For man, "Although he is a traveler in time, he has opened his eyes, for a moment, in eternity." "Christ, the Incarnate Word, is the Book of Life in whom we read God."

There is a subtle temptation to envision Merton the scribe, wistfully churning out popular books of spirituality. But a richer development occurs. We must not overlook the responsibilities assumed and the opportunities for learning taken on by Merton, Master of Scholastics and Master of Novices. It was this teacher's unashamed learning that was frequently reflected in his books. Much Pauline reading and reflection—the cosmic Christ—grew out of his reading the French biblical literature that went into preparation for a course, "Sanctity in the Epistles of Saint Paul," in 1954. Perhaps most important in these resources are the references he makes to the work of Hans Urs Von Balthasar's *La Liturgie Cosmique*. Irenaeus and Maximus the Confessor occupy prominent roles in that study. The familiar themes of the Greek Fathers—"recapitulation" and "divinization"—forecast his next book, a Pauline work dubbed *The New Man*.

As early as 1954, Thomas Merton was writing to his literature professor at Columbia, Mark Van Doren, that he was working on a book about the Greek Fathers which he would entitle *Existential Communion*. The genesis of *The New Man*, as that intended text, evidences a marked maturity in both Pauline thought and the Eastern Fathers.

This volume, often overlooked, is Merton's assimilation of rich theological material. Building upon the Pauline ambiguity about "the world," he traces the existential battle between man's true (spiritual) self *in Christ*, and the false, illusory self (agonia). The cosmic Christ of Paul and the "recapitulation" theories of salvation of the Eastern Church are evidence of Merton's becoming steeped in their Christology. Most of all, Merton resists the Promethean mysticism—an "error" he called it—that takes no account of anyone but the false Self.

This same Christological reflection comes to bear on the work that I consider his single most significant volume for spirituality, *New Seeds of Contemplation*. Revisions of the 1949 text are almost entirely reflections on Christ. It is perhaps almost systematic. Chapters twenty-one, twenty-two and twenty-three express much of this redaction of Christ-reflections into the revised volume. An enormous Merton transition is found in the summary chapter, "The General Dance." It summarises the Incarnational maturation in Merton's spirituality. The humanity of God resounds in these pages:

> The Lord made the world and made man in order that he himself might descend into the world, that he himself might become man. When he prepared the world he was about to make, he saw his Wisdom as a Man-child, "playing in the world, playing before him at all times." And he reflected, "My delights are to be with the children of men."

And so he surmises, "The presence of God in the world as its Creator depends on no one but himself. His presence in the world as man depends in some measure upon men." But he quickly adds: "Not that we can do anything to change the mystery of the Incarnation in itself; but we are able to decide whether we ourselves, and that portion of the world which is ours, shall become *aware* of his presence, consecrated by it, and transfigured in its light." He concludes, "The world and time are the dance of the Lord in emptiness." He invites us to "cast our solemnity to the winds" and join the cosmic Christ, transforming all creation.

That may sound quite Dionysian, indeed! But a sobering element of that optimism remained in the next transition of Merton's spirituality. He signaled it early in 1960, in the Preface to *Disputed Questions* and his introduction to *The Wisdom of the Desert*. The perspective was that of "Christian Humanism and Personalism." Merton grew uncomfortable with the idea of the monk as one who "takes flight from the wicked world and turns his back on it completely in order to lose himself in antiquarian ritualism, or worse still, to delve introspectively into his own psyche."

It was in large part the drama of his correspondence with Boris Pasternak and the ordeal of the 1958 Nobel Prize offered in unfriendly Russia that drew Merton into the crucible of humanity in his own era. The voice of monastic protest was stirred to witness. He identifies the single theme coursing through the book (a disparate collection, incidentally) as the relation of the person to the social organization; more traditionally put, solitude vs. community. Merton resonates with the protest of *Doctor Zhivago* as religious, aesthetic, and mystical. While Pasternak was not a "Christian apologist," Merton discovered a great affinity. Pasternak's vision is "essentially Christian."

> That is the trouble: the problematical quality of Pasternak's "Christianity" lies in the fact that it is reduced to the barest and most elementary essentials: intense awareness of all cosmic and human reality as "life in Christ," and the consequent plunge into love as the only dynamic and creative force which really honors this "Life" by creating itself anew in Life's—Christ's—image.

> It was not until after the coming of Christ that time and man could breathe freely. Man does not die in a ditch like a dog—but at home in history, while the work toward the conquest of death is in full swing; he dies sharing in this work.

Dehumanization—man alienated from his history, death like the dog in the ditch—this exposure gripped Merton's sensitivity. In *The Wisdom of the Desert* he reappraised his monastic "involvement" with the world. The monk is the most hospitable of men, he affirmed. He helped the world recover from its illusory, egocentric self to live "in Christ."

The charter for Merton's turn to the dehumanizing plague that throttled the world of the turbulent 1960's— that arena of moral crisis—was being written in the Second Vatican Council. Merton was an enthusiastic observer. In his eclipsed volume, *Redeeming the Time* (a British edition in 1965; parts are reprinted in the 1965 American edition, *Seeds of Destruction*), Merton addressed this new attitude of the Church *toward* the world. *Gaudium et Spes*, the Constitution on the Church in the Modern World, he remarked, found the Church now "prepared to recognize that the secular world in its very secularity has values worthy of honor, and that men who have nothing to do with the Church and her faith may still be helping the human race to advance towards its spiritual maturity."

He analyzes Karl Rahner's notion of the "Diaspora" Church as a moment of great choice, an affirmation by the Christian world. And in what seems to be one of the "Copernican revolutions" Rahner discusses, Merton himself begins to consider "grace" outside the scholastic categories of "obediential potency." He surmises: "Christian anthropology is not yet fully clear about the person, since what belongs to the whole Christian person has traditionally been ascribed to the *soul* (part of the person only) and to grace. The Christian theology of grace needs to be reviewed in the light of a new and deeper metaphysic of the person and of love." That was indeed the project *in process* in Merton's own thought. Merton suggests that "so personalistic is the humanism" of Vatican II that the Constitution on the Church in the Modern World might be renamed "The Human Person in the Modern World." "It sees the meaning both of the human person and of the whole family of man in the light of the Incarnation."

Little wonder that by the time of his next important book, *Raids on the Unspeakble* (1966), he confesses that "I love you the best" to his essays in a lyric prose. The citation of Gabriel Marcel inscribed at the opening of the volume pierces in its clarity: "Today the first and perhaps the only duty of the philosopher is to defend man against himself: to defend against that extraordinary temptation toward inhumanity to which—almost without being aware of it—so many human beings today have yielded." Quoting Berdyaev in the prologue to the book, he speaks of Eschatology not as an invitation to "escape toward a private heaven: it is a call to transfigure the evil and stricken world"—the good world where Christ dwelt and is still present among us. So the Patristic tone of his appeal: "Guard the image of man, for it is the image of God."

The fully-human had become the arena of God's humanity in Christ. Merton's protest against dehumanization flowed from his Incarnational spirituality, whether in the searing impact of his "Letters to a White Liberal" in *Seeds of Destruction*, where he addressed the American race war, or on Vietnam in the same pages, or the essays on *Faith and Violence*. It was this experience of Christ as God's transforming humanity, revealing to us the fullness of our human condition (suffering and glory) that plunged Merton into the social criticism current.

Perhaps nowhere was he more insistent upon resisting dehumanization than in the essay, "Rain and the Rhinoceros" of *Raids*. The dilemma of "mass man" versus the person, of solitude versus community, was imaginatively presented in the Ionesco character who yields to the herd mentality, the lowest common denominator of humanity. The stampeding man in the rush (rhinoceros) refuses to see solitude as the threshold of charity. The solitary of the city or desert, Merton warns, "is not so armored; he favors mankind with reminding it of its true capacity for maturity, liberty and peace."

In his extraordinary essay in the same book, "The Time of the End Is the Time of No Home," Merton concentrates a magnificent reflection on Christ. I think it is one of his most poignant. In a rare, consciously eschatological theology, he speaks of the opposition between the secular anxieties that tend toward a hope for a *violent* end and an eschatology that is "revealed fulfillment."

"When the perfect and ultimate message, the joy of which is *The Great Joy*, explodes silently upon the world, there is no longer any room for sadness." "All things," Merton says, "are transfigured" in the coming of the Word. He deepens this examination of Incarnation. In Christ, the "fullness of time" comes to the world. "And it is necessary that there be no room in the inn—there has to be some other place. In fact, the inn was the last place in the world for the birth of the Lord." This scene of Christ's birth is amid the "time of the Crowd," mass man. The Word is spoken amid a "display of power, *hubris*," the census, the amassing of humanity (the whole world) for registration, numbering, "identification." "For what purpose?" Merton asks. Taxation and military conscription in the Empire.

> It was therefore impossible that the Word should lose himself by being born into shapeless and passive mass. He had indeed emptied himself, taken the form of God's servant, man. But he did not empty himself to the point of being mass man, faceless man. It was therefore right that there should be no room for him in a crowd that had been called together as an eschatological sign. His being born outside that crowd is even more of a sign. That there is no room for him is a sign of the end.

To a world of rumor and noise, the bazaar of census, the kerygma of indeed "Good News" came. In poverty. "Christ comes uninvited," Merton records. Resisting the temptation—a "demonic" one—Merton speaks of true eschatology as not "end" but "the final beginning, the definitive birth into a new creation." It is not the last gasp of exhausted possibilities, but the first taste of all that is beyond conceiving as actual." He ends with the question: "But can we believe it?"

Merton's voice in the arena of special criticism questioned the old patterns that the religiously-oriented layman *endured* "in a good way" by living a simulated monastic life "in the world." That baroque and medieval *external* monasticism had dissolved in favor of the monk as a "marginal man," in dialogue and conversation with the world.

In the newly-embraced Diaspora Church, Merton set about re-working his spirituality. Perhaps nowhere did it better manifest his reappraisal than in his ecumenical explorations. While we cannot venture into the Asian studies in this chapter, I do find that his dialogue with other Christian theologians matured his own devotional reflections on Christ. It was, indeed, a long way from the *Mountain's* dogmatism (one writer recently termed that early Merton as "bigoted"!) to his interaction with other Christological thought. It is no coincidence that he would quote approvingly from Karl Barth, "Tell me how it stands with your Christology and I will tell you who you are."

In *Conjectures of a Guilty Bystander*, a collection of journal pages from the late 1950s and early 1960s, Merton offers a book "not . . . of professional ecumenism, but a personal version of the world" in the 1960s. There is transparency and again the unsystematized flow of Merton's thought. In *Redeeming the Time*, Merton refined his monastic renewal: It is not arrogantly to bring the world to submit "to the feet of Christ in his traditional and familiar aspect (the Christ painted on wood and covered with gold in the sanctuaries)." Rather, Merton notes, it is a monasticism "which hopes the living Christ will reveal himself in these meek ikons of flesh and blood, hidden in the world, solitary and humble men of prayer." The monk himself had come to embody what Merton had first glimpsed in those ancient mosaics—iconic presence, a hopeful sign of transformation.

The overture to *Conjectures* Merton entitled "Barth's Dream." The anecdote about Barth's dream of Mozart's reply to his Protestantism belongs to some of Merton's most memorable pages. Mozart's accusations against a Protestantism "all in the head" captures both Barth and the Gethsemani monk. Barth is, Merton summarizes, "Unconsciously seeking to awaken, perhaps, the Sophianic Mozart in himself, the central Wisdom that comes in tune with the divine and cosmic music and is saved by love."

The centrality of Incarnation in Barth's own theology is paramount. Reflecting on Barth's 1931 Christmas sermon, Merton delights in what he discovers. He identifies with Barth's affirmation that the Light born at Bethlehem is "certainly *the most unprincipled reality one can imagine.*" And the identity between both writers is forged in Barth's query: "Is perhaps an unconditional faith in all sorts of principles not the typically German form of unbelief?" He agrees with Barth's insistence on the character of Revelation—Incarnation is a primary art of *gratuity*, not to be explained by reason, but responded to in faith as "gift." He had also admired Barth's earlier work on Anselm, *Fides Quaerens Intellectum*, in which Barth insisted on the tradition that the Incarnation is not a juridical reality (soteriology) but differs from that "ransom" theory popularized by Augustine. The mystery and theology of the Cross, Merton concurs, take their meaning not in terms of blood vengeance but as a mystery of *love* united with justice. Interest in Anselm's *Cur Deus Homo* drew Merton's enthusiasm. As Merton points out, his medieval favorite, Duns Scotus, "is in many ways a disciple and interpreter of Anselm."

The affinity for Barth's work is rooted in this rich terrain. Certainly the 1965 work, *The Humanity of God*, by Barth, drew upon the depths of a common vision. It is necessary, as Barthian scholars point out, that Barth elected to speak of the "humanity" of God and not his "divinity." For Barth, God's relative qualities—omniscience and power—can be sacrificed. Two absolute qualities, the absolute *authority* of God and the *love and freedom* of God are maintained when God presides over the whole human condition in humility. In the Incarnation there is the freedom and love of God that permitted him in all humility to be for us "God for a second time" as Barth would phrase it.

Merton tempered his reading of Barth by also noting some points on which he disagreed (without specifying them). There would most certainly be an uncomfortableness with Barth's Calvinism, his conviction that the finite is ultimately incapable of the infinite. In this sense, Barth's Neo-Orthodoxy confronted Merton's more thoroughly Incarnational confidence. The image is used of Barth's Christology that depicts the Incarnation as a "tangent," not penetrating the human condition, but merely contacting or intersecting with the circumference of humanity. Nevertheless, the primacy of God's Word in love, God's humanity, riveted Merton's attention.

If Barth was a discovery for Merton, the work of Dietrich Bonhoeffer was a revelation. While Barth would speak of transformation of persons "in faith" by *religious* categories, Bonhoeffer addressed the transformation of the world in *human* categories. His appraisal of the human was far more confident than Barth's. Merton's optimism thrives in the dialogue. He quotes from Bonhoeffer in the epigraph of Part Two of Conjectures:

> . . . The news that God has become man strikes at the very heart of an age in which the good and the wicked regard either scorn for man or the idealization of man as the highest attainable wisdom.

Christendom, Merton said, must recognize the "embarrassing truth" of "the world into whose history the revelation of God as man broke through, profoundly modifying all human structures and cultural developments." Quoting from Bonhoeffer, Merton repeats: "the humanity he accepted was, and remains, in all truth, *our* humanity." The plague of false spiritualism takes us on an escalator to unworldliness. Rather, Bonhoeffer oriented us back to a true Christian "worldliness." The Christian choice was "simply a complete, trusting, and abandoned consent to the 'yes' of God in Christ."

The conscientious opposition which Bonhoeffer elected in resisting Hitler's machinations, Merton says, scorns a

Church grasping for a merely temporal, worldly sense of survival, which denied the symmetry of our lives with the Cross and the Victory of Christ and his Resurrection. Bonhoeffer's "Christian worldliness" and "religionless Christianity" is not, Merton stresses, to absolve the world from all guilt. That is the tangent of some of his disciples whom Merton scolds—the Radical Theologians whom we will address momentarily. Theirs is a free-wheeling and breezy optimism, misdirected. Bonhoeffer's "worldliness" Merton locates as God's presence "in the world *in man*," an elementary New Testament teaching from I Corinthians 3:17. Merton returns to Pope John XXIII's *Pacem in Terris* with its anthropocentric focus, man "sanctified in the Incarnation." The very great threat, a threat resisted and reversed by Bonhoeffer, Merton insists, comes from a reversal of the meaning of Incarnation: "Man's refusal of himself."

The Bonhoeffer dialogue ignites new dimensions of conscience in Merton's monastic protest. In fact, I consider that the re-evaluation it catalyzed (provoked?) is perhaps one of Merton's most searching final ordeals. His reading notes of Bonhoeffer date especially from the time of his "retirement" to the hermitage at Gethsemani, in August, 1965. It is so beautifully ironic that his struggle with Bonhoeffer's "worldliness" should coincide with his eremetical nativity. The main text from Bonhoeffer he reads at this juncture is the *Ethics*. In the midst of refining a sense of "social responsibility," Merton unearthed Bonhoeffer's critique of "medieval monasticism" and the accusation that it is a misunderstanding "escape" from the world. I consider that the title for his new volume, while perhaps already in Merton's imagination (cf. his essay, "Letter to an Innocent Bystander" in *Raids*) owes much to Merton's wrestling with the imprisoned German Lutheran pastor.

In a notebook selection dated October, 1965, Merton pauses to become introspective and searching. It explains the aptness of a repentant, converted "monk" who comes to embrace the world ever more boldly. He entitled the lengthy excursus: "My place in the world." "Obviously in my early writings I said things about 'the world' that had a gnostic or manichaean flavor about them." He goes on to say that he no longer accepts such statements, but there is a sense in the tradition that gives a basis for them—the "negative view" of "the world" that balances with the positive in the New Testament. He goes farther to specify his "anti-worldliness" as that of genuine medieval monasticism, not the reactionary stance of Pius IX's "Syllabus of Errors."

"I think my writing is split into two categories as regards this question. 'The world' seen in terms of nature, of manual work, of literature, culture, Asian philosophy, etc. etc., is fully *accepted*. Also 'man' in his historic reality. What is not accepted—the world in its contemporary confusions." At which point Merton admits not having faced the technocracy and the crises of contemporary culture with anything but pessimism. Perhaps as his own harshest critic, he continues: "There may be more truth in my pessimism, but the pessimism itself has an evil root, and instead of getting the root out, I have been cultivating it in the name of 'spirituality' or what you will. This is no longer honest. My task is to come to terms *completely* with the world in which I live and of which I am a *part*, because this is the world redeemed by Christ—even the world of Auschwitz." There can be no compromise with Auschwitz, Hiroshima, or Southern racism, he insists. But, on the other hand, "they too must be 'redeemed.' The great task of redemption is in America, which imagines itself Christian! That is why I am here, and must stay here."

No longer relying on the "God of the gaps," as Bonhoeffer phrased the inadequate theological legacy, Merton turned his appreciation of the German revisionist of secularity to the project of contemporary Radical Theologians, the American idiom of "God is Dead" theology. We must note that his appraisal for it bears on his reflections on Christ. While the diagnosis of J. A. T. Robinson (author of the precipitous *Honest to God* volume) and company, earned Merton's sympathies as an appreciation of "diaspora" Christianity, he read the movement as theologically lame. Essays in *Faith and Violence* endorse their diagnosis of the contemporary faith impasse without subscribing to their claim to be descendants loyal to Bonhoeffer. It is the "absolute religious keneticism" where Christianity is even emptied of God that halts Merton. He scolds the Radical Theologians for what he dubs "the death of history" (and therefore the loss of biblical eschatology) and finds them stopping at the Cross. God does not rise again "to resume his former transcendence," Merton surmises. He remains only as immanent, empty and hidden in man and in the world."

It is worthwhile to note that Merton finds Thomas Altizer's *The New Apocalypse* redeeming the radical theology by relying on William Blake's work. It is not surprising that Merton's own appreciation of Blake would rally some common bond! However, in summation, we must ask whether Merton's reading of the directions of Radical Theology and its Christ were reliable. The subsequent work of Robinson, especially this New Testament scholar's *The Human Face of God*, presents a Christology of God's "Man for us" that resonates strongly with Merton's own reflections on Christ. Indeed, we must face the prospect of Merton's failure to appreciate the movement and his narrow response recommending apophatic mysticism as the eclipsed theology for which Radical Theology searches.

It is in this same light that we make an evaluation of Merton's somewhat terse and limited reading of Pierre Teilhard de Chardin. The surprising note is that while both Merton and Teilhard are grounded in the Christology of the Greek Fathers (a transfigured creation), they never entirely converge. At least Merton's hesitant and half-hearted recommendation of Teilhard disappoints. His reading of and familiarity with Teilhard seems limited. An unpublished review article of *The Divine Milieu* as well as the record of his reading DeLubac's *The Religion of Pierre Teilhard de Chardin* are major resources. Though he would applaud Teilhard as "the symbol of the new Catholic outlook upon the modern world," and praise him as the one who "can speak the language of contemporary man without totally compromising his faith in God and in Christ," Merton's aversion to the system of science aroused a marked hesitation. It smacks of the same Barthian aversion to "principled reality"—undermining the gratuity of the Incarnational God. And yet Merton can gravitate to an appreciation of Teilhard that is enthusiastic. Teilhard's perspectives are Paul's "recapitulation of all things in Christ," the cosmic Christ:

> The radiant focus of all reality is not only the Divine Being, but God Incarnate, Jesus Christ. The Spirit of man exists for Christ. But material things exist for man in Christ. Not . . . (as) obstacles . . . He gave himself to us in matter sanctified and sacramentalized. . . . (This is the) sublimely eucharistic heart of the spirituality of Teilhard . . . . the mystical Christ (and not merely) the Risen Lord dwelling in heaven.

In his commentary on Albert Camus' *The Plague*, Merton ventures his most direct critique of Teilhard. While we remember that in Bangkok Merton would acknowledge the Marxist enthusiasm for Teilhard and his great contribution, Merton has resisted the scientist's alleged devotion to an idea, a mystique, a system. Camus, he said, had also protested the sacrifice of man in his present condition to the lure of an ideology attracting him to some "future." Teilhard, he judged, opts for "an optimism which tends to look at existential evil and suffering through the small end of the telescope," unable to scruple and anguish with Camus over the murder of an innocent child, but able to glory over the new atomic-powered bomb without pausing over its human toll. Perhaps as revisionists appraise Merton on Teilhard, they will want to search for more convergence between these two poets of twentieth-century Christological reflections. Indeed, this hesitation about Teilhard will seem harder to defend.

Our panorama of Merton's ecumenical dialogue on Christ demands one other cursory glance at an integral partner, the Greek Orthodox tradition. A student of the Greek Fathers, it is no surprise to find Merton's research and enthusiasm for contemporary Orthodox spirituality. Bulgakov, Meyerndorff, and Schmemann are prominent in his reading. Alexander Schmemann's *Sacraments and Orthodoxy* captures the essence of the tradition in Merton's late readings. He reviews the book and announces it as "my legacy" to the novices, as he retires to the hermitage in August, 1965. In the book he sees "life as 'cosmic liturgy,'" . . . man as restored by the Incarnation to his place in that liturgy, so that with Christ and in Christ he resumes his proper office as high priest in a world that is essentially liturgical and eucharistic."

But most notable is Merton's appreciation of the transformation that lies central to the Orthodox tradition: again, it is the sense of the icon as mediating God's humanity. It is here that Merton expresses one of his most direct reflections on the Cross as integral to the Paschal Mystery. Christianity often appears—Merton quotes Schmemann—"to preach that if men will try hard enough to live Christian lives, the crucifixion can somehow be reversed." However, we cannot evade or ignore death, or neutralize the force of the Cross. The victory of Resurrection is *through* the humility of the Cross, which declares Christ's presence *in the world* as resurrected Lord. This is a distinct affirmation of the secularists' great truth which Orthodoxy renews.

Finally, what about the poetry of Thomas Merton? I have reserved this problematic and neglected dimension of Merton's work as the climax to our appreciation of Christ in his imagination. Failure to come to grips critically with Merton's poetic talent scandalously eclipses the essential Merton. Much Merton scholarship will be revised in the future as this dimension comes into more competent research.

Jean LeClercq attributes the resilience of Merton's message to its "dynamism,", a force in motion. By "trials, thrusts, break-throughs," Merton effected vigorous spiritual renewal. This is the very pattern of his maturing poetics.

While he declared "monastic silence a protest," he went on to identify his speech as a denial "that my faith and my

Church can ever seriously be aligned with those forces of injustice and destruction" marshalled for dehumanization. The voice of Merton's protest perhaps most powerfully resounds as a Christic consciousness in the much-neglected poetry of this talented Trappist. In this regard, to turn to the poetry of Merton, we observe the familiar thesis of Romano Guardini, that artistic imagination precedes theological reflection by a decade, even a generation. Merton's meditation on the Incarnate Christ exercised a profound influence through his poetry.

The regeneration of Christianity finds a loyal ally in poetry. Over the years, Merton's own mature confidence in the humanistic art grew stronger. He gained momentum as a poet. Certainly there is a development from what George Woodcock styles the "poetry of the choir" to the "poetry of the desert." But each is etched with that "incarnational stoutness" (as Nathan Scott likes to term it) which radiates a transfigured humanity. In one of his early poems, "Song for Our Lady of Cobre," Merton remarks how the inspired lyric set him on a path of similar poems for several years.

This is a kinetic poem, flowing with motion, almost choreography. Meditating on the Black Madonna of Cuba, the virgin of devotion, its simple transition from black to white urges a rhythmic meditation. There is, in technical terms, much immaturity in this poem's reliance on simile ("like" recurs throughout the poem). But the cosmology of the poem reflected in the "ring of stars" points to the Christ event as transforming the earth. This is signaled in the "pieces of the mosaic, earth" getting up and flying away "like birds" Although naive in its expression, the confidence in transformation and the very apt image of the mosaic's intricate pattern draws our memories back to those mosaics in which Merton discovered the Christ—as we noted at the beginning of our discussion.

Images of transformation inhabit Merton's poems. But always the dynamic is that of Incarnation, the full *humanization* of persons and the earth process. Creation is worthy of God's Christ. Indeed, in this strategy Merton reflects much of what Kierkegaard rehearses as God's "journey toward us," a most apt revelation of the fully human. Perhaps Merton's most famous poem, "For My Brother, Reported Missing in Action, 1943," thrives on such metaphors (not the simpler similes!) of transformation. And the humility of God on the cross of suffering and death embodies this fully incarnational dynamic in John Paul's death and Merton's transformed consciousness.

The spectrum of the early (pre-1960) poems includes many selections which involve the participation of children. I most admire poems like "Dirge for a Town in France" (apparently quite autobiographical), "Aubade: Lake Erie," "Advent," and "Winter's Night." Later poems will also be populated with their innocent presence, a new creation. There is a sacramental presence in their "mimosas in the window" of the wives of "Dirge for a Town in France." The women in the "traceries" of their "aquariums" look down and preside over the world of children whose imaginations stand in stark contrast to the lethargic husbands who prowl in shadows, mocking the inevitable loss of innocence by children. But Merton—here borrowing heavily from Rilke's "Carousel"—suggests that the children's world of imagination, transforming vision, is more *real*. It is the paradise-world that a transformed consciousness, effected by the Christ, invites. There is almost a pre-occupation with the "window" as the vantage-point in these children's poems. It takes on great meaning with reference to Merton's essay, "Poetry, Symbolism, and Typology" in his meditation on the Psalms, *Bread in the Wilderness*. In that early work Merton depicted the poet as reporting on the objective world as "redeemed." The poet observed and imaginatively re-presented that world, which he, like Adam, viewed from the window of his room. The sections of *The New Man* which reflect on Adam as "re-created" find Merton attributing to the poet Adam's office of "naming" things. It is a holy and sacred vocation. Indeed, the poet creates a "calculated trap for meditation" (DeRougement). The attitude of the children in "Aubade: Lake Erie" offers a transformed vision that replies to the hoboes whom morning finds tracking to the wail of the "wood winds of the western freight." (Fine alliteration, often missing in the sound of Merton's poetry.) They fail to see the wheat and grapes of the Lake Erie northern regions, "an artificial France," as transformed into eucharistic Bread and Wine. They are the dehumanized, abandoned debris of Industrial Revolution, called by these children to greet the day with a transformed eye—not as "a hundred dusty Luthers."

The dynamic of illusion and reality weaves through Merton's poetry. With irony and a searing compassion, Merton traces the spiritual pilgrimage in his poetic imagination. It is no accident that his own literary background was so matured and polished by the Columbia University contact with Mark Van Doren. And the currents of the New Criticism as a literary charter merged happily with Merton's incarnational consciousness. Indeed, the two are happily juxtaposed. Interestingly, Merton's first published book review in the New York papers was of John Crowe Ransom's *The World Body*. There prospered a confidence in the poem as a "verbal icon" (as William K. Wimsatt captured the sense of this critical theory in his book of that same title).

The Christ of Merton's devotion and the "objective correlative" principle of the New Criticism converged. There was, Merton demonstrated, an *intrinsic* relationship between the objects presented by the poet and the emotions they specified. Perhaps the finest example of that success in Merton's short poems arrives in "Night-Flowering Cactus," a poem Merton's friend Bob Lax has dubbed "his spiritual autobiography."

The landscape of "desert" dominates the geography of the early monastic centuries. It declares the "marginality" of the monk. But more, its poverty, aridity, and isolation (solitude) are the environs for the dynamic of transformation. So the first stanza images the protean hiddenness of the cactus' identity. There is a sacramental quality in this cactus' quiet praise, lifting its "sudden eucharist" out of "the earth's unfathomable joy." The images of void, poverty, and "virginal thirst" are in harmony with the "world body" which is mosaic-like in its intricacy and wholeness. The quality of "mystery" (*sacramentum*) is simultaneously to reveal and to conceal. So the yawning "white cavern without explanation" becomes the silent bell in the next stanza. The echo of that contemplative union with God transforms. Quietly, silently, isolated in the solitude of the desert, the cactus flower ("bell," too) blossoms.

In the emptiness and barrenness of the desert, the "impeccable" humanity of this personified cactus offers its poignant beauty. In darkness and void, the fragrance of the flower lures. Once again, the "bird . . . flies" from the mosaic of the desert's earthen tones. It is reminiscent of those techniques of icon painting, using only earth's elements, pure, unadulterated elements like the egg and natural pigments. They are transfigured in the corona of gold. The fully human figures are transformed into a third dimension of spirituality by the affirmation of earth.

In later poems Merton was even more successful in similar mosaics of earth, in part because he was not so directly allusive to the religious category (e.g. "sudden eucharist") but creation became declarative in itself. "Song for Nobody" with its "yellow flower," a "golden heaven" and "gentle sun" is liturgical in its "light and emptiness." The very "uselessness" of its presence and beauty and the solitude it presents express the spiritual dynamic of Merton. "O Sweet Irrational Worship," where the "Wind and a bob-white and the afternoon sun" are personified; an almost Hopkins-like imagism is achieved. The refrain, "I am earth, earth," moves Merton's confidence in the earth process even further.

We cannot overlook that enduring portrait Merton wrote into poetry in "Grace's House." The child Grace's crayon drawing inspired a spiritual meditation. Its child-like detailing and the out-gazing of animals and Grace herself ("From behind a corner of Grace's house. Another creature peeks out!") remind us of other "windows" in Merton's poetic myth. The poet's playful ambiguity about

the "river" ("No, it is not the road—Alas, there is no road
to Grace's house!") inaugurates his hymn:

> O Paradise, O child's world!
> Where all the grass lives
> And all the animals are aware!
> The huge sun, bigger than the house
> Stands and streams with life in the east
> While in the west a thunder cloud
> Moves away forever.

For Merton, Christ-consciousness, the affirmation of
our fully-human arena of God's presence, is a paradise-
consciousness. Not in some nostalgic, sentimental back-
ward glance, but in a transforming experience.

The articulateness of Merton's own critical measure
of other poets affords us the insight into his poetic project.
In a review of the work of musicologist-poet Louis Zukofsky, he has offered one of his most enlightening and revealing statements. The review was entitled "Paradise
Bugged." He opens "All really valid poetry (poetry that
is fully alive and asserts its reality by its power to generate
imaginative life) is a kind of recovery of paradise. Not that
the poet comes up with a report that he, an unusual man,
has found his own way back into Eden; but the living line
and the generative association, the new sound, the music,
the structure, are somehow grounded in a renewal of vision
and hearing, so that he who reads and understands recognizes that here is a new start, a new creation. Here the world
gets another chance . . . another start in life, in hope, in
imagination."

It is this mythic vocation of the poet that Merton discovers in his own monastic identity. There is a kindred
religious dimension in the poet's work. An article on
"Symbolism: Communication or Communion?" in 1968
testifies to this ability of the symbolic imagination to
"contain in itself a structure which awakens our consciousness to a new awareness of the inner meaning of life and of
reality itself." This Zen-mindfulness is an attention to things

in their identity. It dissolves illusion. Symbols are "in themselves religious realities in their own right," says Merton, "especially when their nature is sacramental."

He delights in the speech of Zukofsky's many children, "a paradise speech" that addresses things "familiarly" because it is not alien and "anticipates nothing but joy." So Merton describes Zukofsky as his "favorite Franciscan." The "paradise ear" must hear Zukofsky's poems. "In fact they cannot be heard except against the vast background of silence and warmth . . . His poems do not make sense except as part of the whole creation that exists precisely for love, for free, for nothing, unnecessary."

There is not space to explore the change in Merton's poetics when he announced that they were "on vacation" with *Cables to the Ace* and *The Geography of Lograire*. Suffice it to say that they continued to probe and meditate on the fully human and the sacramental quality of life. The idiom changes abruptly into "anti-poetry" which Merton employed as a tool to shock, cajole, and feed back static to the culture, parodying its deprivation and advertising jargon. It became a matter of salvaging the word, piece by piece, so that "language itself would get another chance."

Cables offers the best imaginative construct with the dehumanized Caliban as foil to Merton's imaginative world. The interfacing of Shakespeare's *The Tempest* and Miranda's "Brave New World" are keys to *Cables'* interpretation. With both this and the following lengthy work, *Lograire*, Merton refers to their structure as being "mosaics."

The chronicles of dehumanization recorded in the cantos of *Lograire* are an odyssey of the world's spiritual consciousness, portrayed with searing compassion. They witness Merton's tenacious confidence in the humanity of God and his protest against the heresy of Docetism wherever he found the mystery of Incarnation compromised. Indeed, these last testaments, the lengthy poems, are his most problematical but sustained imaginative ventures on Christ. As a "mythdream," Merton's poetry sought to help us, as he phrased it, to "decode your own scrambled message." As he searched the "Cargo Cults" of the Pacific and their myth declaring human relationality, he proclaimed the humane factor: "We two fit like the two halves of a cockle shell." That transformation of consciousness, catalyzed by the poet's imaginative construct, presents anew the Christ mystery.

As Merton himself remarked, in summarizing Zukofsky's poetry, "The real subject of the poem—of all his poetry—is . . . an anticipation that is aware of itself as a question." The poet shares the reality "of that question . . . in a way . . . in which it cannot provoke any answer that would appear to dispose of it. So we never go on to the next question. Each poem is very much the same question, but brand new," a venture back to ultimate questions. This conviction Merton wrote into his poem, "Elias—Variations on a Theme." Let us end with its meditation, a suggestion that Christ is that recurrent mystery for the spiritual pilgrimage.

> Here the bird abides
> And sings on top of the forgotten
> Storm. The ground is warm.
> He sings no particular message.
> His hymn has one pattern, no more planned,
> No less perfectly planned
> And no more arbitrary
> Than the pattern in the seed, the salt,
> The snow, the cell, the drop of rain.
>
> The free man is not alone as busy men are
> But as birds are. The free man sings
> Alone as universes do. Built
> Upon his own inscrutable pattern
> Clean unmistakable, not invented by himself alone
> Or for himself, but for the universe also.